BREAKING THE RULES

A fresh approach to building on the strength and courage of our struggling youth

Irv West

Cover art by Maggie Graf and Liz Parsons.

ISBN: 978-0-615-64902-3
First printing: September 2012

FOR INFORMATION CONTACT:
Irv West
661 High Street
Athol, NY 12810
518-623-3987
Cell: 518-636-9653

Please visit his website below
where online ordering is available:

www.irvwestyouthadvocate.com

Printed in the U.S. by Morris Publishing®
3212 E. Hwy. 30 · Kearney, NE 68847
800-650-7888 · www.morrispublishing.com

DEDICATED TO
ELEANOR AND SAM

They alone taught me that I had worth.

Table of Contents

Introduction

Yesterday I spoke with a friend who told me how her daughter, a first grader, was yelled at by the teacher because she was fidgeting in class. The next day her mom was called into school and was told her child had emotional problems and needed testing. The words stung this mom and drove her to near panic. "What did I do wrong?" "Will she be all right, or is it too late?"

I was furious when I heard this because I know the child well, have talked with her many times and watched her play with her friends. I know there is nothing wrong with her. At most, you might say that she has abundant energy, is curious about everything around her, and enjoys physical activity. Perhaps that's the problem. It is easier to teach children who are passive, so those who aren't must be made to be so.

I have watched this scenario unfold all too often, and I know what comes next. After the recommended testing comes the diagnosis. She will probably join the disturbingly large number of people diagnosed with Attention Deficit Hyperactivity Disorder or ADHD. Psychotropic medication is then prescribed, and the child has her healthy energy all bottled up by chemicals!

There is a kindergarten teacher I know who loved her kids and loved teaching them. She taught for 17 years. At the annual meeting with the principal before the beginning of the school year, she was told that her children would not be allowed recess this year. "Why?" she asked incredulously, "Because the time is too important. We've got to prepare them for first grade."

She told the principal that she herself could not go without recess, so she was not about to ask her five-year-olds to do so. When he made it clear that this was non-negotiable, she resigned and forfeited much of her pension.

�

A friend of mine is a psychologist. She was told that her son was behind in his language development. (He had not yet begun to speak at the time that the developmental charts decreed it should happen.) They agreed to an evaluation and they were told he may well be early Asperger's. As a psychologist, she knew this was erroneous because all the other symptoms were missing, so she ignored the alert. When her son was ready, he began to talk.

✖

A teacher frequently screamed at her kindergarten class where my friend's child attended. The child became frightened and, on a couple of occasions, wet her pants. (This had not happened before she began attending this class.) The principal suggested therapy and special classes. Mom was not a fighter and was easily intimidated, so she gave her consent. After a couple of sessions, the possibility of employing psychotropic medications was introduced and, again, mom consented.

I fear for the future of this child, as much as I fear for other children who are subjected to this screaming teacher. In their eagerness for this girl to get therapy and drugs, they never looked at causative factors –

namely the teacher being ill-suited to her work or, at the least, in need of guidance.

⁂

There is a family with whom I am acquainted who was told that their son had multiple problems, including brain damage. (There is seven times more frequent diagnosis of brain damage among Black children . . . and their son is Black.) They also said he is easily distracted, plays at a premature age level, has language difficulty, and is late crawling. (He later got up and started to walk, skipping the crawling stage entirely.)

Today he is a ship's captain, so I doubt that he is easily distracted (at least I hope not). He is a social being (they said he was antisocial), articulate (they had diagnosed him with a speech defect), and living a truly fulfilled life with a wonderful mate. None of this could have happened if the conditions they found had validity.

⁂

I remember sitting on a committee mandated to plan an all-day workshop for high school students about stresses in the lives of young people. I was excited about the concept and suggested that I bring some of my troubled youth to the next planning meeting to give our planning meaningful context.

A social worker on the committee said: "Irv, you can't do that. They are not qualified!"

Troubled youth not qualified to speak about the stresses of youth? Really!

I brought them anyway, and their insights were invaluable, because they kept us grounded in reality.

You might say that I lived up to the title of this book and *broke the rules*.

I could give many other examples.

What's wrong with us? Have we gone insane? Have we lost sight of the needs of our young people? Aren't we supposed to meet their needs, not have them comply with ours?

These youngsters are crying out to be understood as much for their hopes as for their fears, for their inner strengths more than for their outer behavior. We parents, counselors, therapists, teachers, and neighbors need to learn how to listen to them!

Time and again, the schools, detention facilities and even therapists have rendered the futures of our young people inaccessible. When you turn a young person into a chronic, legal, drug addict you decimate their future. Lecture them as a substitute for listening to them, and you create distance. They shut down. Focus your efforts on correcting what is wrong with them, instead of building on what's right, and they taste defeat.

These kids whom I have come to know so well through their struggles have grown to trust me with their deepest fears, their most heart-wrenching depression, their uncontrollable anger. They have also shared with me, and still do, their inspired writings: poetry, music, and stories.

They want – no, more accurately, they need – to share their feelings with others outside their own circle, in the hopes that they will be recognized for their courage, their humanity, their need to feel connected to their community, and for their sharing of the same goals we all have – to lead a meaningful life.

I have felt privileged to be trusted by these youngsters. More often, they are self-protective and flee from people (and situations) that make them fearful – not unlike that of a deer running from a hunter in the forest. They have been hurt too many times and are no longer able to trust openly. They have also developed the skill to quickly and accurately identify dishonesty and they respond accordingly. That they have trusted me speaks to their recognizing my deep caring for them. Hopefully, after you have met some of these youth, you will care too.

I have wiped away too many of their tears, listened to too many of their angry words, looked in the eyes of too many saddened souls, to sit passively by anymore. I need to give voice to their being. This is their voice . . . this is their book!

What Adolescents Need

As a framework for understanding their world, I will tell you three things I have come to know that these youngsters have been lacking, but desperately crave.

1. A Continuity of Caring: Many of us were fortunate enough to have grown up in an intact home. Our parents cheered us on in our quest for fulfillment, comforted us in defeat, and were there to reign us in when we drifted from responsible behavior. Every child needs an adult to be there for them, with them . . . not for a few days, or weeks, or even months, but until their lives are on track, and their goals are clearly defined and within reach. They need a place that is safe and predictable, a place of nurturing.

But that's not what kids in the child care system get. They often have foster care workers and detention workers who say they care, but only while on the clock; they have others who come in and out of their lives, briefly caring, then disappearing. They recognize the falsity of these claims to care, so they grow suspicious and shut down . . . or act out!

They often receive therapy from more than one counselor. It is called the "silo effect." Money is targeted to solve a specific problem, like aggression, drug abuse, or alcoholism (one day we will realize that alcohol *is* a drug). Each agency provides funding for treatments targeted to their specific raison d'être, and each funds a therapist. Worse, as these children are shuffled from home to home, from facility to facility, they have to start all over again with a new therapist. They have to pour their heart out to a total stranger. I remember doing an intake on a girl and asking her if she had been seeing a therapist. She said she was seeing *three*. I asked if they were helping, she leaned forward, and said, "Mr. West, they are driving me crazy. They all tell me something different."

How can we morally justify, in the name of funding streams, confusing this 12-year-old girl. As I spoke with her, I realized painfully that now that this girl was in detention, far from home, she would be assigned a brand new therapist, and would have to start from the beginning . . . with another total stranger!

When considering the basic needs of life – food, housing, access to health care – studies have shown that people consider having a home to be the most critical. No matter how inadequate it may be, having a place of retreat, of security, of solitude, of predictability, provides a setting for all other problems to be resolved. Something kids in the system are denied.

In the detention facility where I worked, counties would contract a bed, thereby assuring its availability when they needed it. When it was not occupied, the facility was permitted to make it available to other municipalities. So, if the facility was at capacity, and a contracting county called in the need for a bed, a youth from the "general population" had to be transferred out. It didn't matter how well they were doing, or even if they had responsive parents who lived nearby and visited regularly. They were transferred! One girl, whose parents were there every visiting day, was sent more than 200 miles away . . . with only a couple of hours' notice!

2. An Island of Strength: We all have it.

You know what it is – that consuming passion, that eagerness to know more about something, to want to spend your life in it as a career. It decides what books or magazines we read in leisure, dictates our hobbies, and helps define our being.

That passion is still there for struggling youth, but it has become so seemingly unachievable that it gets buried in their subconscious. With support and encouragement, it can be brought to the surface and become a life motivator.

Because so many of these youngsters have no conscious vision of a future, they turn to immediate gratification. They drug out, booze out, act out. Some become depressed and, in extreme circumstances, attempt to end their life. (The alarming rise in adolescent suicides is reason enough for us all to be concerned, and move us to action . . . to reform.) Others simply withdraw. To respond meaningfully, we first have to listen, to really hear them.

When someone is not able to visualize a tomorrow, it is not hard to understand why they want to extract as much gratification as they can from today. Really, wouldn't most of us change our lifestyle if we were told, for example, that we had 3 months to live? I know I would. I haven't smoked a cigarette in more than 40 years, but if given word that I had no tomorrow – let's say I had terminal cancer – I would rush out and buy a pack of cigarettes at once. No, I would buy a carton of cigarettes.

When a child's *island of strength* is identified and nurtured, almost magically the weight of their anger, depression, and frustration is lifted. Instead of looking at the pain of the past, they begin to envision a future rich with dreams, hope, fulfillment.

3. A Connection to Community:

We all have a connection to our community, sometimes through simple acts like babysitting for neighbors, other times with broader involvements like volunteering in a hospital, fighting for civil rights or for world peace. It is a good feeling to be a part of a larger whole – to work for the common good.

Our troubled youth are too often deprived of the opportunities to feel part of the dynamic of life that is unfolding all around them . . . to feel connected to that surge of life . . . to that energy.

If a youngster feels he is being ostracized by society, he gets angry and withdraws. It is a self-fulfilling prophecy because then society condemns that child for being antisocial, disturbed, often attaching a diagnosis or two.

No child willfully seeks out punishment, nor does any child want to reject recognition and praise. Yet troubled youth often act out in ways that bring them just that – reprimand and punishment. Why?

There are certain protective mechanisms that we all possess. They prevent our pain from reaching a level greater than our tolerance to bear it. Safety valves for those who have been deeply hurt in the past tend to be more extreme, and may include severe bursts of anger, self-imposed isolation from society, even ending one's life as a means to finally be free of the pain. When the pain eases, the burden of protection diminishes, and the need to self-protect becomes inconsequential. It is at that critical time that we must be there for them, reaching out and providing support, nurturance, helping them to connect with their community . . . their world.

✖

How to get the Most out of This Book: As you enter each child's world, try to suspend all preconceived ideas and beliefs. Also, try not to draw comparisons with your own children, others you know, or even your own childhood experiences. Each child is unique, is growing up in his or her own time, and deserves your undivided attention.

Hayua, often referenced in the letters section, is the Japanese word for peace. I taught it to all of my kids and often have it shouted out to me in the streets by them.

A Couple of Disclaimers: Names of the youth have been changed, as have locations. In some instances portraits and stories are composites. This was done to further protect anonymity, and in the interest of conserving space.

Only minor editing was done to the poems, out of respect for the (mostly) teen authors.

Voices of our Struggling Youth

KARA

Kara grew up in a drug ridden, poor neighborhood and attended an overcrowded and understaffed school. She had trouble coping with the school work and got no help -- so she truanted. She was labeled PINS (person in need of supervision) and was sent to detention.

Kara was angry . . . angrier than any other child I had ever met. She approached every person, and every situation, from a posture of suspicion and resentment. Offer to help her, and she would flip you off. She had been hurt so often that she created barriers of protection all around her. No one was going to be able to hurt this girl ever again! At 14 years of age, and sporting an afro reminiscent of the 60's, Kara's life had already seen more hardship than someone three times her age.

On a Saturday morning we all sat down to enjoy a large breakfast that I had prepared. There had been a horrendous racial incident reported in the newspaper that morning, and I mentioned it to the kids. (Kara was Black-Hispanic, and was there with a White boy and Black girl.) I commented that we have come a long way, but still had a long way to go.

Kara glared at me (she had a wickedly potent glare) and said, "I live it; I don't need to hear it!!" This girl had no intention of being reminded of the prejudice she had been subjected to in the past.

I changed the subject.

Later, when we had cleaned up and were preparing to go on an outing, I asked the two girls to come into the kitchen. Kara glared again and, anticipating some kind of reprimand, said, "What did we do now!!" (The staff usually only talked with the kids privately if it was related to a disciplinary infraction, so Kara was quick to assume that was my motive.)

I explained to the girls that I worked in Selma, Alabama during the civil rights movement and witnessed some horrible racism. Also, my wife is Black and still suffers oppression. I said to Kara, "But I should have been more sensitive to you and I apologize."

Kara looked at me out of the corner of her eyes and, in a doubting tone, said, "You apologiz'n, Mr. West?"

I looked back at her from the corner of my eyes and, imitating her tone said, "Yea, Kara, that all right?"

Kara looked at me dead on, and said, "That's cool, Mr. West. No one's never done that to me before."

In fourteen years, no one had apologized to this girl for a mistake made, a word misspoken in the heat of the moment. To Kara, adults were this rigid body stuck in their ways, ruling with authority, not willing to discuss or negotiate anything. And here I was "apologiz'n" for something I had said that was insensitive.

Slowly, Kara learned to trust me. She would gradually talk about her life, her fears, and, – hesitantly at first – her aspirations. She would challenge me respectfully, advocating not only for herself, but for the other youth there with her. She won some battles and lost others. In its own time, and at her own comfortable pace, her walls of protection came tumbling down.

I saw her once after she left, at a responsive long-term home for girls. She was studying in the school library when she spotted me. She ran to me screaming,

"Mr. West, Mr. West, and hugged me." Then, with great enthusiasm, she told me of her plans for the future, which included college. There was excitement in her voice and an eagerness to share. Even her afro seemed to have grown larger.

A teacher came out of a nearby classroom to see what the ruckus was about. When I apologized for the distraction, she said, "Oh, you must be Mr. West. Kara told me about you. It's all good, it's all good."

I did not hear from Kara for three years. It is not unusual for a child to look ahead, rather than dwell on their sordid past and the people who, even in a helping way, were a part of it. (Still I would always give my mailing address and cell phone number to those youth who asked for it – a clear violation of boundaries but a strong statement in support of "continuity of caring.")

One day, from out of the blue, I received a letter from her. She wrote that she was graduating from high school with honors, and had been accepted to a nearby college. She went on, "I am not perfect . . . I still get angry sometimes, but I remember what we talked about and I use it in a good way."

What is Kara really telling us . . . beyond her words? *Those dialogues with Kara were possible only after she had been exposed to my vulnerability, my humanity . . . through my apology. And that came about because I looked past her anger, really heard her pain, and understood her need for self-protection. Adults in her life would see the anger, but not look beyond it. They never did understand that the anger was little more than protection from the pain.*

Kara lived in a very poor community where, all around her, dreams of a fulfilling life were being drowned in the immediate gratification of drug and alcohol highs. She resisted those temptations and tried to achieve in a school that was understaffed and underfunded. She got little meaningful help and grew progressively more frustrated, more angry.

Kara had no one to talk to, no one to care, no one to take her hand and guide her to the right path.

The system that was intended to be of support to her, instead did Kara wrong. There is no logic in taking a girl struggling with school out of that environment and putting her in detention for weeks. When she returns to school, she is that much further behind, has no new coping skills, all of her classmates know where she has been, and she is subjected to ridicule by her peers. Yet I met more youngsters remanded to detention for truancy than for anything else. It is also fiscally unsound! For the more than $700 a day it costs to keep a child in detention that child could have been given tutoring <u>and</u> counseling while in school.

COLORBLIND

I have reached to touch the sky,
and it melted down bleeding into my eyes,
technicolor lies to make the world beautiful.

The cracks in the sides pass under my feet,
watching them quiver a giant maw of teeth,
as it opens wide and swallows all that was left of me.

Flipped over the fence to see,
if the grass was really green,
only to notice everything was grey.
This gentle beat

BREAKING THE RULES

Like traffic on the streets
slow and easy; impatient driving faster.

This, this feeling a disaster,
I told you this would never last,
and just like the sky bled into my eyes,
as I slipped between the cracks into the confines,
where even the lies could no longer reach.

Well I'm just here to teach.
There could have been more than this.
Isn't sorrow bliss.
I'd be lying if I say I didn't miss,
The way you cried when you realized this.

The gray grass gave me light in the darkness.
And a pair of bright eyes
and soft hands to touch my heart.
Makes it beat faster.
The smile ever plastered across my face to start.

To know you had the chance;
only to withdraw from the dance.
There is light in my dark eyes.

-- Mecanna Beah Karin
(pseudonym), A Teen

SARIETTA

Sarietta, like Kara, was there for truancy. She skipped school, and hung out. Not with friends, she had only a few. She would go to the library and write poetry – at least a poem a day. And she was not only prolific, she was a talented poet.

She was not good at relating to adults. She would withdraw and fall silent. Her primary means of communication was through her writings, not conversation.

One night, the kids were all going to bed and I was helping to settle them down. I looked in the room with Sarietta and her roommate and said, "Good night my children." I might as well confess right here that I am really bad with remembering names and, because of the closeness that so many of these kids felt to me, they often took my forgetting their names personally. Calling them "my children" was both comforting to them and obfuscated my problem with remembering names.

The other girl (you guessed it, I can't remember her name) said, "Good night, Mr. West," but not a word from Sarietta. I looked directly at her and said, "Good night my other child." She looked at me, smiled (I had not seen her smile before), and said "Good night, Mr. West."

That evening I noted in the staff communication log that Sarietta was reachable, but at her own pace. I explained what had happened at bed time.

The next day, after the director had read the previous day's entries, she wrote a reprimand: "No terms of endearment!"

It is hardly worth mentioning that, when there were children the director liked, she would call them "sweety," and another staff person, a friend of hers, called them "hon." The point is that, while it was not my primary purpose, these kids did need to hear terms of endearment. It was new to them, it warmed them, it made them feel wanted.

Sarietta slowly started to talk to me about her life, the worthlessness of her existence. Now that communication had been established, I suggested that I get some of her poems published. She spent many evenings selecting the ones she felt best suited for publication and revising them. What better way for her to be acknowledged than to be a published author.

In the meantime, I discussed this with the director, who said she would need to get her mother's permission. For the next few weeks I asked her regularly if she had contacted Sarietta's mother. She said she was too busy. She could have more accurately said she was too apathetic.

Eventually they were published, using a circuitous route.

What is Sarietta telling us . . . beyond her words? *When a child's self-esteem cannot be elevated with words, you meet them in a place where they are comfortable. For Sarietta, having her poems published gave credibility to her writings, and did wonders for her self-esteem. No spoken word from me could have accomplished as much. But it couldn't have happened before she learned that she could talk to me . . . that it was safe to talk to me. That took time, patience, and meeting Sarietta in her own "place," her writings.*

�֍

Alter Ego

I find myself lost in swirling mists,
their magnetic pull impossible to resist.

Try as I might I cannot escape,
When I look into your eyes this is my fate.

My protective shell weakens under your intense gaze,
All of my emotions flare up in a searing blaze.

No one else could scratch this diamond hard wall,
and only you can see to its fall.

Far beyond those layers of shields
lies an inner core ready to yield.

So if it is your desire to know the true me,
Your eyes will have to look deeper than what they see.

-- Cruise Dittus, A teen

�֎

LEONORA

Leonora came from a highly dysfunctional, single-parent home. The house should have been condemned for its unsanitary conditions. She and her two sisters were given no parameters of behavior; they would often stay out all night, and their mother would hardly acknowledge their absence.

On a couple of occasions, Child Protective Services investigated, but the child was not removed, nor was help provided to the family. There was no father in their lives.

Leonora had a long history of being placed in detention facilities and ran from most. I met Leonora when she was remanded by the courts to our facility for truancy.

She spoke freely about her depression, but never about hope for the future. There were few friends in her life, and her all-consuming concern was basic survival . . . living day to day. Ask her what she wanted for her future, and you got a blank stare. Future? There was none, only a lonely existence today.

Each day at home mirrored the previous one – truanting from school, getting away from her home environment, sitting on park benches when the weather permitted. Hardly a life worth living.

She ran from us during an outing at a local park. She was quickly caught by the police and returned to the park where we were waiting. The officer in the car informed me that since she had threatened suicide, they were required to take her to the mental health unit of the local hospital.

I asked to speak with her and received a puzzled expression from the officer that I interpreted to mean, "Why bother, you're not responsible for her anymore?"

I persisted.

Leonora was in the back seat, her face covered with tears, her body tremulous. Through her deep sobs, she apologized to me for running. Then she asked a favor.

"Mr. West, there is a quilt on my bed at detention that my grandma made for me. Could you arrange to get it to me? It means so much to me because she is dead now." I assured her that as soon as my shift ended, I would personally bring it to her at the hospital. She thanked me, and they drove off.

When I returned to the facility, I relayed the request to a facility supervisor, and told her of my promise to deliver the quilt when my shift ended. She responded that I am absolutely not to take it to her. "How else will she learn that what she did was wrong? She has to learn!" I was mortified but felt powerless. The director (and most of her assistants) were intimidating people and exercised absolute power over the staff. I never spoke up to them, even here, where I was being forced to renege on my promise to a girl very much in need. I fell silent and at shift's end went home in tears.

It was far from the first time I ended my shift with either a heavy heart or an all-consuming feeling of rage.

The quilt was put in the basement – in cold storage.

I saw Leonora twice more, once when she was being arraigned for a small burglary (I sat in the visitor section of the court as a statement of support, but she didn't see me), and again on the street a few months later. It was then that she told me she had done some prison time for a small burglary which, having been in the court that day, I already knew.

She also told me she was staying out of trouble, but nothing more, nothing positive, still nothing about a future, still a lonely existence.

What is Leonora really telling us . . . beyond her words? *During that poignant moment in the back of the police car, when Leonora's life was crashing in on her, she turned to the memory of her grandmother for support, for sustenance.*

To suggest that Leonora needed to "learn a lesson" is to imply that she was in full control of her behavior.

Leonora ran because of an all-encompassing fear, not the free-will decision to violate rules. We presumed experts often do not differentiate willful behavior from what Leonora exhibited -- the need for self-protection, to flee from seeming danger. We would do better if our efforts centered on exploring the child's underlying need, rather than the surface behavior. Only then would we be able to identify Leonora's island of strength, provide her with counseling and, together, nurture her future.

She was crying out for life affirmation and needed help to acknowledge her own self-worth. Once her island of strength was identified, she would no longer sense danger . . . and no longer need to run.

At all the more responsive long-term detention facilities I visited, a concerted effort is made to get something personal, something of value to the youngster, something they can keep in their room. I have seen rooms of the angriest, seemingly toughest youth with teddy bears on their bed. Others have photographs, special letters they received, jewelry with sentimental meaning. The symbolic value of having this link with home must not be underestimated.

My boss once told me that she and I would never get along no matter how long we worked together. "I am punitive, and you are responsive," she said. She was right. I wanted to responsively return the quilt to this broken child, and she saw to it that it was withheld as punishment.

I wanted to ask her how a cello could be any more of a weapon than the chairs the kids sat in, or the knives they used to cut their meat. I wanted to tell her about the musicians I have known who would not even let me touch their instrument for fear that the oil on my fingers would affect the instrument's tone. I wanted to plead with her to permit this shy child to present her cherished instrument – her *island of strength* – to her peers. I wanted to question why she felt that a girl who had not previously demonstrated any aggression toward others would do so at a time of fulfillment for her.

Instead, I went out and told Marsha of the change in plans and watched her eyes fill with tears.

What is Marsha telling us . . . beyond her words? *What an opportunity was lost by rejecting Marsha's simple request. People, who are shy, doubting their own worth, will often recognize a strength in themselves through a talent they have, much like Marsha did with her cello.*

This girl, who was clinging to a semblance of dignity through her island of strength (she had never been away from home before and was scared), had it stripped away. A weapon? Musicians cherish their instruments,

Music is also an important means of communication between youth. In the facility where I worked, youth were not permitted to sing. "They might send gang signals," I was told.

Dreams of Destruction

I play a solitary symphony,
frowning in misery and playing long sad notes.
Darkened halls, no stage lights shown,
a lonely figure all alone.
Empty hall echoes and shadows dance with the sound,
notes swirl in a whirlwind around.

The strings, non-existent betray my array,
of carefully calculated music.
The silence it stays,
just beyond earshot away,
when the dull roar turns to a single clap.
The sound of the bow hitting the ground,
and the click of the case as my violin is put away.

Perhaps someday the light will shine,
until then this empty stage is mine,
and just like the wind i am gone,
with my empty notes following on the breeze.

-- Mecanna Beah Karin
(pseudonym), A teen

SOULETTO

She was a Black girl from an urban area, who had just been transported more than 50 miles in the back of a police car in handcuffs and shackles and she was terrified! It all happened because she had skipped school.

32

The detention home was located in a rural area with an almost all-white population. The racial configuration of the staff pretty much mirrored that of the community, as did the population of youth remanded there. When we received a Black youth, they almost certainly came from a city a good distance away that had a high-Black population.

Many of the youth, regardless of where they came from, were scared when they first arrived, not knowing what to expect. But it was harder for those who stood out by race and who came from further away. Souletto was terrified. She had never been away from home, never been in trouble, or rarely (if ever) been out of her all-Black neighborhood.

What is it like to be pulled out of your familiar neighborhood, taken by police patrol to a strange place where it is truly dark and quiet at night, where your parents are out of reach? How do you react? To truly understand how this girl felt, you might want to imagine yourself in a comparable situation. If you are White, picture yourself taken to a facility in an all-Black neighborhood with all-Black staff, an alien environment from which you have no escape.

Souletto was crying hysterically, banging on the walls and windows frantically. It was near evening, and I was concerned about being with her and having minimal evening staff. The administration tried to arrange a transfer (I am ashamed to admit that I asked them to), but was unsuccessful.

She left the next day, somewhat calmer, to points unknown.

What is Souletto telling us . . . beyond her words? *A strange setting can be frightening. Every* attempt must be made to bring a child comfort through familiarity.

We only had one Black person on our staff. She had offered to come in voluntarily in a situation like this, but she was not called.

Staff (myself in this instance), needed to allow time to have its calming effect. She was much more comfortable the next morning, less fearful for her life, so there is every reason to believe that things would have worked out. I was too eager to request that she be transferred . . . too fearful of her hurting herself. I was fearful for my own safety as well, and it was irrational. This poor child was terrified for herself, but was not at all aggressive to others. I overreacted.

A wise person said to me in a training class, "Be where the person is." I have practiced that while running a home for terminally ill, working with troubled youth, serving in a nursing home. We should have been where Souletto was and had our one Black staff member come in and make her comfortable in a way that we could not.

✖

Shattered Dreams

He grew up on the streets in a small family
But when he turned twelve they moved to Tennessee
He felt alone in this strange new place
He was the only one with a colored face
He didn't yet know about discrimination based on race
But soon his life would take a change of pace

The first year wasn't half bad
He got called names but wouldn't get mad

BREAKING THE RULES

He didn't mind sitting alone in class
Being separated from the mass
He often yearned for the life of his past
When people didn't try to break him like glass

He couldn't understand why he was treated like this
Some people acted like he didn't exist
He tried to fit in but was constantly rejected
This was prejudice to which he was subjected
He thought time would put an end to this feud
But when he joined football it began anew
His prowess in the sport was clearly seen
No one could beat him on those 100 yards of green
The other players' jealousy grew
Their pride hurt, they gave him
what they thought was long overdue
That night with four touchdowns
Their target won the game
When he walked home would be when they took aim

Walking down the street alone
Shadows jumped with minds of their own
The three came in front and three from behind
In a flurry of twelve fists he became entwined
A blow to the head engulfed him in darkness
His life was now forever gone into this eternal abyss

One teen dead, six others on trial
Two parents that will never again see their child smile
A little tolerance could prevent this devastation
Prevent one death and six incarcerations
It's a lesson that everyone should act on
Race is the last thing someone should be judged upon

-- Cruise Dittus, A teen

35

✷

SOLSO

Solso had 9 brothers and sisters, all either in detention or prison. Both of his parents were incarcerated as well for selling drugs. He was sent to detention because of an altercation at another detention facility.

Ironically, Solso never used drugs or drank alcohol. This 13-year-old boy, who exercised daily, said he respected his body too much to introduce chemicals. He followed all the detention rules and never received a warning of any kind, but did not participate in any of the group activities. No ball playing, no board games. He never talked of a future, not even what's for dinner. Put food in front of him and he would eat it, tell him when to go to bed, and he would go. He lived entirely in the moment.

I took the kids on outings regularly to avoid confrontations. These kids would not normally socialize with each other and idle time was often a precursor to fights. I also enjoyed exposing them to new worlds – experiences they might not otherwise taste in their lifetime.

So it was that on one beautiful Saturday, we headed to a goat farm renowned for their goat cheese. There were 140 goats, also llamas, and a mix of rescue animals. The farm owners were friends of mine. I had brought many youth there in the past, and they were all welcomed warmly.

One of the owners greeted us, promptly excused herself, then returned carrying a two-day-old goat. She walked right up to Solso and asked if he would hold it while we toured the facility. That was the first time I had seen Solso smile, with the goat nuzzling his neck. He cradled this fragile life form in his arms, gently rocking it as you would a baby. It was like a religious painting, warm and spiritual . . . loving. Solso looked so different, the tension drained from his muscular body.

Back at the facility, I was sitting on the living room couch with only a few minutes to my shift ending. Solso walked up behind me and speaking to himself (but surely wanting me to hear), he said, "I don't care where they send me next, I just hope they have animals there." He was talking of a future for the first time, even if it was one built around the assumption of another placement.

Solso was transferred without notice to a facility hundreds of miles away. Kids were frequently moved about like chess pawns to suit the needs of the system. It was a very one-sided game with the system always winning, the kids losing. I have seen so many children of very caring parents suddenly transported out of reach, severing (at a critical time) their nurturing bonds of support.

That evening the owner of the goat farm called me at home to tell me that she would like Solso to work there when he got out. I wrote and told him. He wrote back almost immediately, a letter full of excitement (another first) and said that he would move to the area and ". . . definitely work there."

I replied, assuring him that the job at the goat farm would be held for him. I encouraged our staying in touch with each other and included some small talk about the weather and about my animals. The letter was returned, unopened, marked "rejected by facility."

Solso's dream of a future had been severed by what was ostensibly a helping agency.

It should be noted that letters to youth in detention are read by staff before being given to the youth. This letter was not read by anyone; it was not even opened!

I was never able to communicate with Solso again, and I am sure he thinks that I lost interest in him. As happened so often in the past, I felt powerless. I contacted the state licensing agency and was referred to the ombudsman, who asked me to send him details in a letter. I did that same day, even including copies of my communications with Solso – especially the one the facility had rejected.

I never heard from the ombudsman again.

As I write, I am aware that Solso has turned 18, and has almost certainly been released. What happens next? His one dream went unfulfilled, and all of my attempts to contact him have been unsuccessful. Where does he go, if not to the streets? To prison? What other options does he have?

A couple of my letters to Solso appear at the back of this book, including the one rejected, so you can decide for yourself whether it should have been passed to him or, alternatively, have him protected by withholding it.

What is Solso really telling us . . . beyond his words? *When a child has been hurt so often and so deeply in their past, they become self-protective. A caring person must work hard to win their trust and their heart.*

It often happens through a common safe ground and, here, it was the animals. They provided that neutral, non-threatening connection between Solso and me – it was the beginning of trust, of a bond between us. It also gave Solso a reason to believe in a future.

Regulatory agencies, like those that oversee youth detention facilities, carry the burden of protecting those in their care. But that must not be at the exclusion of encouraging safe nurturing relationships from outside the system. Solso had identified his island of strength and was learning to trust. Who knows where he is today. What is known is that by rejecting my letter and breeching our dialogue, the agency sent the wrong message to this young man who deserved much better . . . he deserved a life!

Solso was cast aside by the rigidity of the system. If he grows progressively more angry, we have only ourselves to blame.

During the early period of his stay with us, I took Solso on a hike – an easy, little known trail that opened on to a beautiful landlocked pond. My boss discouraged it because of the isolation but finally relented.

We were out of range of cell phone coverage and, about midway to the pond, Solso said, "Mr. West, I feel funny inside." As an old arthritic EMT, out of cell phone range, the image of carrying this strapping boy out was disturbing.

"Solso, what do you mean," I asked in a quivering voice.

"Mr. West, it feels quiet inside me . . . strange."

It was the first time this boy had ever felt peace.

John Muir wrote: "Climb the mountains and get their good tidings. Nature's peace will flow into you as sunshine flows into trees. The winds will blow their own freshness into you, and the storms their energy, while cares will drop off like autumn leaves." Solso had just discovered peace . . . for the first time.

"I think I could turn and live with animals,
they are so placid and self-contained.
I stand and look at them long and long."

-- *Walt Whitman*

✂

The Butterfly

I pick open the lock on my solid chamber door,
slowly drifting carelessly across the floor,
when something wondrous appeared
and caught my eye,
unlike anything I've ever seen before.

I open the window,
and to my hand would appear,
a beautiful butterfly shining and clear,
I blink a few times to wash away the dream,
but the butterfly is much more real then it seems.

I well up the courage,
and hold the butterfly close to my lips,
a single kiss to betray all that is real today.

I have seen my butterfly flirting about others faces,
and it was then when I deny,
perhaps I never truly thought we'd see eye to eye.
The smile broadens,
and the night grows thin,
I release the butterfly to her sweet somber dreams,
and close my solid door and await again,
for the one I've missed.

In bliss we dream even on lonely nights it seems,
I am the wind to carry your tired butterfly wings.
and my heart sings, for you tonight.
Tonight . . . goodnight.

-- Mecanna Beah Karin
(pseudonym), A teen

�֎

FRANK, JOSE, RAFAEL

During the early part of my tenure at the detention facility, school was conducted in space rented in a nearby church. The building was unoccupied during the week by anyone but us, and we used one of a number of classrooms on the second floor.

I took the kids to class whenever I was not held back for a reprimand from my boss. It was my choice because it got me away from the administration and kept me with the kids. On one occasion, I transported Frank, Jose, and Rafael – each of whom hated the other. It was a volatile mix.

Soon after class started, all fury broke out. Words were cast, and I knew it would be a matter of time before fists would fly.

I separated the kids, putting one in each vacant classroom. As I stood in the hall, not letting any of them peer out from their respective rooms, I called for "reinforcements." While I was waiting, I thought of those arcade games where you stand with a soft hammer and hit the figures who, unpredictably, pop up out of holes. But I had only words ("get back in that

41

room!"). Soon a counselor arrived and, with two vehicles, we split the kids up as best we could and headed back to detention.

I asked the kids to sit down in the living room, and we talked. There was no reprimand, because it was an uncontrolled outburst that stemmed from uncontrolled emotion. My goal was to help them recognize that there were alternatives to how they handled their anger and aggression. I asked them what happens when they start to get angry. One said he grinds his teeth; another said his body feels heavy; the third told the group that his fists involuntarily clench.

Then I introduced the possibility of being aware of those reactions when they first occur, and getting away from the precipitating circumstance as soon as they could. (We had already all agreed that nothing good comes from these altercations.) I was so engrossed in the conversation that I did not hear the facility director come out of her office and stand directly behind me.

Suddenly, in a booming voice, she yelled, "This is going in my court report . . . you are all going to pay for this."

The conversation abruptly ended. We returned to school, this time with two counselors to keep the peace.

Another time, the director had said to me about herself, "I don't handle stress well."

What are Frank, Jose, and Rafael telling us . . . beyond their words? *These kids have heard threats most of their lives and have grown immune to them. Trying to help them realize there are alternatives to their behavior is so much more effective than random screaming. Once a child has reached full rage (adults, too, for that matter), there is no turning back. But it is possible to stop while the person's reasoning is still* *available to them and that happens in the early stage of an altercation.*

There are times when you really want to lecture. You see the right path, have a clear vision about the transgression, and so want to right things. You might even want to yell! In those situations, it is really important to gain composure and give thought to what would be your most effective approach, which is often at odds with your more emotional one.

When I taught parenting classes, I stressed the need to back away from a screaming match with your child. Then when things calm down, to go back and talk. Nothing good comes from screaming. When emotions are that stressed words are said in anger that are not really meant. When the anger has passed, meaningful dialogue can begin.

Status

Although we walk this earth together
we are separated by forever
love will come and hate will flow
but never will this distance close.

A hollow heart with one cracked layer
Feelings could not become much fainter
Red dust strains through icy veins
Nerves die from too much pain.

Locked away in your selfish reality
You think your life has been all it's going to be.

-- Cruise Dittus, A teen

JOHN

He was a tall, Black, handsome 17-year-old young man, who was uncertain about himself. It was probably exacerbated by his having been transported to a detention facility far from home, from a Black neighborhood to an almost all-White area, from an urban to a rural location, suddenly out of reach of his loving family.

How do you instill pride in a boy who came from a depressed area and attended an overcrowded school with overworked teachers – all in a short period of time?

I brought in a book about Black inventors, and he was enthralled. Most of the scientists had never made it into his school books, and the teachers did not discuss them. The book gave a brief synopsis of each inventor and explained why their inventions were critical to societal improvement. Some were well-known, others obscure.

One that was of special interest to John (I do not know why) was the person who invented the coupling that connected railroad cars. The description explained how there was a desperate need for a simple way to couple and uncouple cars, and it had to be strong enough to withstand the incredible force of the locomotive when it lunged forward. The author elaborated that this was critical to the development of the West – being able to leave a car behind quickly for later unloading and re-coupling of the empty car on the way back.

John said softly to himself, "Wow, a Black man did that."

We went to a local museum that had a painting by the first Black man to ever have art displayed in the White House. We talked about presidents who held slaves, and about racism today. We pondered the strides society has made in recognizing the accomplishments of Black people and the struggles yet to be fought. We talked about how to advocate for change.

He left the facility with a new found pride. He had borrowed the book while staying there and was discharged on my day off. The book was in my mailbox when I returned with a note saying, "Thanks, Mr. West. I feel good."

What is John telling us . . . beyond his words?
There are distortions by all forms of media that are demeaning to minorities. They sensationalize the wrongdoings of a minority individual and often minimize coverage of their achievements. As a Black person, John was not exposed to the accomplishments of his race and, as a result, did not have the self-pride that is a precursor to achievement.

We name schools in minority populated areas after great minority leaders, but rarely work toward instilling racial pride in those same schools. It is self-defeating. Without a strong sense of self, learning is much more difficult. It seems purposeless to the student, partly because they have not been presented with successful role models.

It is no less important to feel a connection to one's past as it is to feel connected to today's community. It is by viewing the accomplishments of the past, that one can visualize the future. In concentration camps during World War II, many survivors clung to the support structure of their Jewish heritage for survival.

John now has pride in one piece of who he is. Let's hope that it proves to be his support and continues to be nurtured by others.

"When someone with the authority of a teacher,
say, describes the world and you are not in it,
there is a moment of psychic, disequilibrium,
as if you looked in a mirror and saw nothing."

Adrienne Rich,
Invisibility in Academe

FRIDA AND ATHENA

Frida and Athena had a playful sense of humor. I came in for my shift at detention one day, and the girls said, "Mr. West, we have to talk to you because we have a problem." "*We* have one?" I responded recognizing the frivolity of their tone.

"Yes, *we*."

"All right girls, talk to me."

"Well, Mr. West, we think that you are a really cool guy. But there's a problem."

"Yes?"

"The problem is that a person can't tell how cool you are until they get to know you."

I inquired if they had a solution to this problem and, of course, they did.

"We want to give you coolness lessons," they explained. "Like the language you use is not cool, and we can teach you better words. Don't worry, Mr. West," they hastened to add, "They will all be appropriate words."

So it was then that I went back to school in the hopes of changing my image and to metamorphose into someone who could be identified at first glance as "cool." In the evening after I had left, the girls would use their free time to prepare my next day's lesson. I was taught the importance of first impressions, what to say and (no less important) what not to say. If I slipped up in the course of the day, the girls would gently remind me of a previous lesson where, for example, I was taught that "hello" should be replaced by "hey." I was even taught how to walk, adding a bit of a swagger to my step. (It hurt my back!)

After a week or so of classes, I asked the girls if I dressed cool. After their laughter had subsided I suggested that we go to the mall so they could show me what I should wear instead. When we returned, I was reprimanded for taking them to the mall. "They could have shoplifted!"

What were Frida and Athena really telling us . . . beyond their words? *We all like being the "teacher," and I always looked for opportunities to encourage that for the kids whenever possible. How often I would say, "Guys, we have a problem. It's my turn to cook, you know I'm a vegetarian, and there is meat on the menu. Kids would jump up and crowd me with their offers to assist.*

"I used to help my grandma all the time, Mr. West, I'm a good cook."

Frida and Athena became my coolness teachers. They loved every minute of it. So did I.

�֎

When you start with the assumption of a child's guilt, you generate resistance, sometimes rebellion. How would you feel if you were accused of something you did not (and would not) do?

There were some children I would definitely not take to the mall, for fear of them shoplifting or acting inappropriately, but not these girls. What happened was that they enjoyed the trust I bestowed in them and responded accordingly. Rather than "homogenize" the kids with an inflexible set of rules, I always responded to the needs of each child as an individual. But that was breaking the rules.

✖

JAKE, CAMILLE, AND NICK

Jake, Camille, and Nick were the only youngsters there on a lazy Friday afternoon. All were well-behaved. Two were there for truancy and the third for a minor drug offense.

The phone rang. It was a woman who explained that she represented a local environmental organization and that the next day they would be opening their new facility. "This is a long shot," she said, "but we need someone to set up about a hundred chairs for the meeting." She asked if our detention kids would be interested in helping.

Although volunteering was not permitted at my facility, I asked the kids anyway (once again breaking the rules, this time by connecting them to community), and they said they would help. Their response was somewhat apathetic, and I suggested that when we were finished we could do some animal tracking nearby.

"Cool, Mr. West," one said.

When we showed up at the location the next day, there were environmental exhibits open to the public. Lots of visitors were moving about and, although we looked at the exhibits as well, the kids were not all that interested. After all, they were there on a mission. They now recognized the importance – the connection to community – of what they were about to do.

The woman signaled that it was time for us to do the chairs – the board meeting would soon be starting. The kids got a look of determination on their faces that I had not seen before, and off they went. They were awesome, lining up each chair with precision. When they were finished, I praised their hard work, commented on the beautiful weather, and suggested we hit the trails.

Nick said, "Uh, Mr. West, we were talking about that while we were doing the chairs. Do you mind if instead of the hike, we stay here and watch them use our chairs?" We stayed for almost an hour, with the kids beaming the entire time. I believe it was the first time in their lives that they felt connected to their community . . . that they were permitted to contribute to society – for the greater good.

What did Jake, Camille and Nick tell us . . . beyond their words? *We too often exclude our troubled youth from participating in their own communities in a meaningful way. Then, when they withdraw to their own tight-knit support system, we condemn them for their isolation. They have the same passion to help that we do, but, for us, there are outlets of expression at the ready, where they are shut out.*

In almost every one of my volunteer endeavors, I have invited struggling youth to help. And every time – without fail – they have shown responsibility, compassion, and genuine caring. They energized me with their commitment!

✄

In my area we have a rebellious group of teens who are called the Juggalos. They listen to anti-societal music and are often condemned in the press. I know many of these kids. When they see me, they come running over to show me a new poem they have written, or music they have composed. They seek acknowledgement, recognition, the ability to share with someone who is interested – someone who cares.

They need a healthy outlet for sharing their excitement, and to revel in their sense of accomplishment, just as much as they need someone to talk to about their frustrations. They need someone who will hear them – someone who cares.

What we should be asking ourselves about the Juggalos is what have we not given these struggling youth that makes them seek out their own all-consuming, rebellious circle of friends. Then we should contemplate how to give them recognition, acknowledgment, a healthy outlet for their expression. Instead, we just condemn, driving them further into a corner. When they feel trapped by someone they feel is an oppressor, they strike out . . . or withdraw from life.

Jake, Camille and Nick would have come alive if given earlier opportunities to connect with their community in a meaningful way. And, by extension, so many others would feel no need for rebellion (other than milder adolescent rebellion – the testing of the waters of adulthood), if they were given that respect.

I remember when one girl, who was helping me organize a fundraiser for a sick family, said to me, "Hey, Mr. West, you are volunteer obsessed. But in a good way."

I am friends with the director of a long-term residential home in a beautiful rural area. When a hiker fell off a cliff while mountain climbing nearby and was seriously hurt, the kids at the home – on their own initiative – put together a fundraiser. They raised thousands of dollars for the family of the man, who had no insurance.

The kids were so happy with the success of the event and with their having been able to help . . . to connect, that they wanted to do fundraisers on a regular basis, deciding as they went along who the recipients would be. The administration was supportive, and it became a regular occurrence. They felt connected. They were the givers, instead of being in the all too familiar role of being the recipients of service.

No Man is an Island

No man is an island entire of itself;
every man is a piece of the continent,
a part of the main;
If a clod be washed away by the sea,
Europe is the less, as well as if a promontory were,
as well as a manor of thy friends or of thine own were;

any man's death diminishes me,
because I am involved in mankind.
And therefore never send to know
for whom the bell tolls;
it tolls for thee.
-- John Donne

❌

ELINOR

Elinor had been wronged by everyone in her life, or so it seemed, beginning with her abandonment by her mother as a young child. She had been a gang girl, had a heart attack when she was 15-years-old by mixing heroin and cocaine, and had no vision of a future. Try as I might I could not identify an *island of strength* for this girl.

Whenever anyone showed concern for this highly intelligent and very charming youth, she would shut them out. She was not about to risk more pain. Vulnerability was something she felt she needed to conceal.

One day I was cooking, and Elinor was watching. I asked her if she would like to help, and she said she would. She took over the kitchen and made an incredible meal. Pasta cooked just right, meat seasoned to perfection, side dishes that many kids would normally not touch – now they were asking for seconds.

I suggested to Elinor that she could go to culinary school, and she said, angrily, "Stop it!" (This was one of many times when my enthusiasm for a child's future took over my better judgment to go slow.) Elinor was not about to let me introduce her to a dream and risk having it pulled away from her at a later time. After all, that was what had happened her entire life.

After some time had passed, I brought her literature about AmeriCorps' culinary program and left it with her to read when she was ready. (AmeriCorps is kind of the government-sponsored domestic Peace Corps program, and their culinary program is held in high regard.) She gradually began to consider it as an option.

In the meantime she cooked. Oh, did she cook!

Finally, Elinor let her defenses slip and agreed to apply to the school. She actually expressed a vision of her future – for the first time!

Elinor had *never* been a behavioral problem for us. In fact, she was the first person to ask if we were going on an outing that day and, if so, where we were going. She greeted every new experience with curiosity.

Then she went for a routine physical, and her doctor prescribed a mood stabilizer, although nothing in her behavior indicated it was warranted. She became lethargic. Instead of asking where we were going, she asked if she could stay behind. She rapidly gained weight, and asked me to stop talking about the school, which I reluctantly did.

She tried to refuse the medication because it made her feel ill, but she was talked down by a facility supervisor. The kids were excluded from participating in decisions about their care . . . they were considered recipients, not participants. There was no effort to even make them aware of the adverse effect of medications, especially not psychotropics. The goal was simply to medicate them into submission.

She stopped talking about a culinary career and, soon thereafter, was discharged to foster care. In my most recent contact with her, long after her discharge, she revealed that she had turned 18 and (by law) was released from foster care. She is now a single mom looking for a job. She briefly reconnected with the gang.

What was Elinor telling us . . . beyond her words? *The best way (perhaps the only way) to contribute to an adolescent becoming a responsible adult is to give them responsibility at as early an age as possible. Elinor was apparently a better judge of whether she should take psychotropics than her doctor, but her voice was silenced. She was treated as an object – a commodity, to be treated authoritatively and to be rendered submissive.*

Of all the immoralities perpetrated on these kids by so-called helping agencies, the misuse of psychotropic medications surely ranks at the top. A recent study showed an inverse correlation between providing helping therapies and administering mood changing medication. Psychotropic medications have become the caretakers of our struggling youth.

Seroquel, a commonly prescribed mood stabilizer, identifies these possible side effects. (This is only a partial list gleaned from the company's own Website):
- *Suicidal thoughts or actions in some children, teenagers, and young adults within the first few months of treatment.*
- *Depression and other serious mental illnesses*
- *Sudden changes in mood, behavior, thoughts, or feelings*
- *Thoughts about dying*
- *Suicide attempts*
- *New or worse depression*
- *New or worse anxiety*
- *Agitation*
- *Restlessness*

- *Panic attacks*
- *Insomnia*
- *New or worse irritability*
- *Acting aggressive, being angry, or violent*
- *Acting on dangerous impulses*
- *Extreme increase in activity and talking (mania)*
- *Unusual changes in behavior or mood*
- *Drowsiness*
- *Dry mouth*
- *Increase in liver enzymes*
- *Long lasting and painful erection*
- *Difficulty swallowing*
- *Upset stomach*
- *Weight gain*
- *Sudden drop in blood pressure*
- *Dizziness*

The pharmaceutical industry is the second most profitable business in the world (oil is first). Drugs are replacing the long-term benefits of therapy which, initially, costs more. However, the long-term administration of psychotropics is enslaving our youth and creating a dependency that, in many cases, will last a lifetime.

The number of prescriptions for mood stabilizers written for children in the United States, increased six-fold between 1993 to 2002, from 201,000 to 1.2 million (Arch Gen Psychiatry 2006). And no age is immune from this horror.

The rate of administration of anti-psychotic drugs prescribed for ages 2- to 5-years doubled between 2000 and 2007. Only 40% of those who were administered the drugs were given a proper mental assessment (Columbia University 2010).

Anti-psychotics were the biggest revenue making drugs of any class, exceeding 14.7 billion dollars a year.

I know of a three-year-old child who was put on mood altering medication because of tantrums. A three-year-old on mood stabilizers because of tantrums!

Medicated

The whitewashed sterile surroundings come up
and smack me in the face.
The cold, collected voices drift to me
and startle me awake.
They tell me these pills i must take,
and i rather admit i enjoy them.

I take them in the morning, and another at night.
Chalk dust slowly turning me into a zombie.
But i kind of like the taste.
Better than the bitter one you left behind.

I peel at the strings that hold my arm in one piece,
little crimson beads come up to meet my fingers
but smear underneath.
So they strap my arms down
so i can't play with it anymore,
and give me a higher dose of the zombie pill.

The world shifts around me,
and i realize i'm being moved.
But then i also realize i am standing and i'm walking
that i'm the one moving me.
The sunlight blinds me,
and i walk aimlessly down the street,

my mind plays pictures behind my eyes,
memories i'd never keep.
I slowly erase it,
and my eyes sink in.
and i never sleep,
i'm just the zombie they asked for.

I'm just another zombie
medicated by society
because they believe i can be perfect
once they crush the real me inside of myself.

-- Mecanna Beah Karin
(pseudonym, A teen)

CAMILLE

Camille was admitted to short-term detention on a judge's remand order because she ran away from home. But it's not that simple. This 14-year-old girl, who has never been in trouble before and was an excellent student in school, lived alone with her father. He frequently would take her to public places like the mall, call her a cheap slut, and slap her. One time he hit her so hard that he broke her nose! Camille tolerated it because it was the only home she ever knew.

When she developed a urinary infection, her father decided she was using the bathroom more than she should, and he needed to "teach her a lesson." He kept her home from school, and told her to get in her bed and stay there until he got back from work that evening. No food, no bathroom. "If you have to piss or shit, do it in your bed," he yelled at her. Then he left for work.

That pushed Camille beyond her tolerance level, beyond her ability to survive in the only home she ever knew and, as soon as her father was out of sight, she ran away. But where does a 14-year-old girl who has never been in trouble before run?

Camille ran to a local supermarket and stole a bottle of hair dye, hoping to disguise herself so she would never be found . . . and never have to return to her dad. But Camille, who was a good student and a good daughter, was a bad thief and she got caught. She was returned to her father, ran again, was picked up and sent to detention.

She did not stay long, and I do not know what happened to her. I can only hope that wherever she went, she got the nurturing that was so lacking in her earlier years at home.

What is Camille telling us . . . beyond her words? *Child protective workers (and family court judges) have among the hardest jobs of anyone. There are different degrees of abuse, and each must be weighed against the realization that removing a child from their familiar home setting, regardless of the circumstances, is traumatic. But when cost saving is permitted to influence this critical decision, the entire process becomes corrupted.*

Clearly, Camille should not have been sent back to her dad, no more than she should have been punished by being sent to detention. By running away from an abusive home, she was making a healthy, albeit short-sighted, decision.

There is something called the "spirit of the law." It is what gives a police officer discretion in choosing an action. If the officer pulls over a vehicle for speeding on a desolate stretch of road, and the driver explains that he was late for a dinner engagement, he would be treated differently than if the driver's wife was in the back seat about to have a baby.

As we learned from mandatory sentencing laws, which remove all discretion from legal authorities, spirit of the law is critical to meaningful implementation. Under these rigid laws, courts are required to mandate a life sentence if there were two priors, regardless of the nature of those offenses. Cause, motivation, circumstances, or even severity of the crime are not considered factors.

The United States has six times the number of people in prison for non-violent crimes as any other country. The only exception is China.

Camille was crying out to not be sent back to the home of her abuser, to have a chance at a good life. The court chose the least costly and most expedient option of returning her to a clearly unfit home. Then they punished her for running from that abusive home by sending her to detention – for stealing a bottle of hair dye so she would not have to go back to her father.

Feels like dying

Just rip it from my chest, the increasing pain
begins to make me blind, vision fading.

Life is nothing but suffering,
and there is no other side,
when i lie six feet in, there is nothing left to see.
Nowhere left to hide.

Four walls will close in,
and the dirt will fill the cracks,
and seal all of my echoes within.
With every passing day,
this pain grows and wears me thin.

Where do i go,
when there's nothing left,
where do i hide when I'm still alive?
where is my other side?

If life is all suffering,
shouldn't there be balance,
a happiness to this chest crushing pound?
Isn't there any happiness to erase the sorrows
that fill every day?

-- Mecanna Beah Karin
(pseudonym), A teen

BILLIE

Billie was obese! Very much so. He had very low self-esteem and would make up fantastic lies that made him seem as important as he wanted to be, but did not believe he was.

When you understand Billie's home life, you can see why. His father was a big man with a dominating ego. He ruled his children with an iron hand, often resorting to physical punishment to achieve his objectives . . . which was to get blind obedience from his kids. He also beat his wife for much the same reason.

Billie retreated, became self-protective, fearful . . . down on himself. It reflected in his doing poorly at school, which enraged his father, who beat him mercilessly, and the cycle kept repeating. No authority at school inquired about Billie's home life, focusing instead on the immediacy of improving his grades. No one linked cause and effect – the hardship of his life with his poor performance in school.

Anger raged in Billie. His obsessive eating did not provide an adequate release of tension. He became prone to fights and, after he really hurt another student, family court remanded him to detention. There Billie deteriorated. Every time he fabricated a story about his life, the kids would challenge him, as did the staff. This exacerbated the problem, ripped harder at his already low self-esteem, and the cycle repeated.

He would not let me plod through his layers of self-protection – enough to identify an *island of strength*. Nor could I involve him in community activities, because he represented a potential physical threat to strangers. There was no possibility of showing continuity of caring, because he was transferred out to a secure facility after he initiated an attack on a peer.

We failed Billie!

What did Billie tell us . . . beyond his words? *Billie's rage, his obesity, and his being prone to tell some whoppers of stories about his life, were all treated in the most superficial way. We addressed his obsessive eating through diet, but never looked beyond the behavior for a cause. Similarly, by challenging his fantastic stories, we embarrassed him in front of his peers, depriving him of any self-respect. In contrast, I ignored the overblown stories and sought out his real accomplishments.*

When someone needs to make up stories to promote themselves, it is usually because their self-esteem is weak . . . in need of bolstering up. And when those distortions are challenged, it tears away a layer of protection and, in its wake, leaves a further damaged and very vulnerable child hiding behind it.

What I did with Billie (what I do with everyone who needs to create an unreal world) is to isolate what is real and nurture it. I let the inflated fantasies fall by the wayside, discarded when they are no longer needed. With Billie, we talked about his superior basketball shots, about the foods he liked, and the music he enjoyed.

After the assault, Billie was transferred to a secure facility. This is like a prison for young people who are incorrigible. The kids march with their hands behind their backs and eyes front; if their eyes wander, they are put in solitary. It is a last resort, or at least should be.

No attempt was made to help Billie, and he is now in a facility where help is not an option.

Untitled

i lost myself among my thoughts,
my never ending abyss,
somehow i feel hollow, like something's amiss
I only wish I knew what it was or where i am,
then maybe i could find myself.
but alas i see the world through another's eyes,
is this truly me or am i in disguise.
i think i'm in someone else's thoughts,
these thoughts can't be mine, can anyone help me?
i'm lost somewhere in time.

-- *Mecanna Beah Karin*
(pseudonym), A teen

✄

ATHENA

Athena was raised in a crack house and was given the option by her parents of selling drugs or prostituting to bring in cash for her "board." She rejected both options and ran away.

Athena recognized that education was the only way for her to build a self-sufficient life. Although she carried the weight of her past and suffered from a debilitating asthma condition, she almost never missed classes.

She was also aware of the importance of having some trusted comrades in her fight for survival . . . a small group of people who had proven themselves worthy. I was privileged to be among them. Another was Elaine, a very caring and responsive school psychologist at the high school that Athena attended.

During her stay at detention, Athena and I would talk about her pain . . . and her future. After she was discharged and back in school, Elaine's office became her safe haven – the place to go when the pressures of her life overwhelmed her and the problems seemed insurmountable. It was a place where she could be reassured that her life had meaning and that a worthwhile future was within reach.

One day, Athena was in the office of her guidance counselor and he said something that got her upset. A student from a more stable upbringing might have shrugged it off, respectfully challenged it, or taken the issue to their parents later that day.

Not Athena.

She recognized the surge of tension growing in her body, left the office without a word, and headed down to Elaine's office . . . her safe haven.

The school knew all about the horrors that had been bestowed on this young girl and her struggle to continue her education. They knew that she had a caring person in Elaine, and that together they could give context to this event. They had the moral obligation to support Athena's choice to move away from the point of stress (we teach the kids that skill in detention), and seek a more comfortable place (be it an actual place, as it was here, or a place of mind).

The guidance counselor chose another course, dictated by the philosophy that each child must be treated the same and made to fit into one mold. He moved into action swiftly, got on his school walkie-talkie, called for both security guards and the school principal to converge on Elaine's office -- on this confused child.

They filled Elaine's office with their presence, blocked the exit, and drove Athena into a panic. Feeling trapped (as she had been so many times in her young life), her place of sanctuary having been violated and her retreat blocked, she kicked at the wall. Probably out of fear for their own safety, they decided to let Athena leave. She ran out of the building, and waited until the situation calmed and she could return to her class. Athena did not want to miss her classes!

At home she had been shut out of love, of nurturing, forced into having to make an immoral and unlawful decision between selling drugs or her body, and it was happening all over again. Only now she was being pushed to fail in a different way, she was being driven out of school. But the outcome would be the same.

Athena was persistent. She did graduate, is in a healthy relationship, and is employed in a job she enjoys.

What was Athena telling us . . . beyond her words? *Athena's school (and so many others) appears to be unaware of the consequences of demanding that each student be forced to act like every other. While it might expedite the teaching process, it creates anxiety and frustration at the least, neurosis at the worst, and can lead to aggressive outbursts.*

Each of us is a product of our past. Only with support and guidance are we able to overcome the bad and build on the good.

Athena had an incredible drive to succeed and she was astute at finding those people who recognized her for her worth. Still, the scars of her past had not healed, and the actions of the school delayed the healing process.

In the end, she was successful in spite of the school, not because of it.

�֎

"Show me a seed and I am prepared to expect wonders."

-- *Thoreau*

✖

BRITTANY

Brittany grew up without any meaningful contact with her mother, and her father had no interest in her. She spent almost all of her young life being shifted from foster care, to detention, to long-term residential placement, back to another foster home. Yet somehow, despite the almost constant shifting, she managed to create art good enough to be exhibited in a highly respected museum. She was awarded a scholarship to art school that, sadly, she could not accept because she was in detention.

Each time she was moved meant new staff to meet, new rules to adjust to and, perhaps of greatest significance, new therapists to relate to. She once said to me, "Mr. West, I can't do this anymore. Every time they move me, I have to start all over with a new therapist . . . tell my whole story again to another stranger."

During Brittany's extended stay at a long-term facility, she managed to earn and save a couple of thousand dollars through a special employment program available to residents. It was enough to attract her father's attention, and he applied for custody.

Brittany was in detention at the time, where we monitored phone calls. So when her father called, I heard him tell her that he was applying for custody. Her dream of living with a birth parent was a possibility for the first time, and she was excited.

"You will have to turn over your savings to me and pay $50.00 a week for rent," he told her with parental authority.

She explained that she had no way to earn the money, and he said, "You are hot and can earn it in one night on the streets."

I reported the conversation to my superior, but do not know if she took it further. I do know that the custody went through. For Brittany it was a life dream about to be fulfilled!

She left promising to keep in touch. (She had stayed in contact with me throughout her institutional meanderings and does to this day.) When I returned to work two days later, my first sight was of Brittany sitting at the dining room table alone, her face covered with tears, sobbing uncontrollably. Next to her sat a plastic water pitcher. No one else was in the room, no staff, no other youth – no one to provide comfort.

I sat down next to her and, together, we sat in silence. It was a bond of caring, of my being there for her – a presence. There were no words that I could have uttered right then to vanquish her sorrow. I didn't even know what had happened and generic statements, like "it will get better," ring false at a time like that.

A short time later, a supervisor came over, looked at Brittany, and yelled: "You are acting like a child, stop it at once!" Brittany swung her arm out and knocked the pitcher off the table. The water spilled, perhaps diluting the tears that had already fallen. The supervisor went into her office and slammed the door behind her. (Later she was promoted perhaps, in part, because of her ability to detect childish behavior.)

After a while, when the sobbing had calmed and the pain had been internalized, I said to Brittany, "I am so sorry you are hurting." She looked at me and replied simply, "Thanks for understanding, Mr. West." Then she got up and mopped up the water on the floor.

Later that evening I learned what had happened. A neighbor of Brittany's father had called the police when she looked out her window and witnessed the father dragging Brittany by her neck through the mud.

That is how her dream of living with a birth parent was crushed; it was why she was crying; the cycle of placements had been reintroduced to her vulnerable life.

What is Brittany telling us . . . beyond her words? Brittany's island of strength was her artistic ability, and her means to achievement could have been the scholarship she was awarded by a prestigious museum where one of her pieces was exhibited. Had the system nurtured this progression, she would have been well on her way to a fulfilling life.

Unfortunately, the system increasingly leans toward the less expensive way, which often stands in sharp contrast to the more caring way. Despite that horrible phone call from her father, it was cheaper to return the child to her parent then it would have been to arrange placement or foster care.

One day, I took Brittany to visit a college that had a strong art department and they gave her an admissions packet. That evening, when it was time for her to shower, she was seen taking the packet into the bathroom with her. A staff person questioned it, and she said, "No one is going to take this dream away from me."

They did, though. They removed the packet, and stored it with her other belongings in the basement. It was a dream interrupted, later to be destroyed.

❋

If I didn't define myself for myself,
I would be crunched into other people's fantasies for me
and eaten alive.

-- Audre Lorde

❋

NANCY

Nancy was 14. She came from a loving household, but something went wrong. We don't know what it was . . . so often it is peer pressure . . . but Nancy was soon using drugs and acting promiscuously.

She followed all the detention rules, was eager to go on outings, and interacted well with the other kids.

One day she called me over and, pointing to a photo on the front page of the local daily newspaper, asked, "Mr. West, what do you think of this picture?" I told her that I thought it was good, and she was obviously irritated by the superficiality of my response. "No, Mr. West, I mean *why* is it good . . . anyone can see that it is good . . . what makes it good?" I had no idea, and asked her to tell me.

Nancy showed me how the lighting and the angles highlighted those aspects of the photograph that supported the accompanying story. She was right!

To my wife's consternation, my next step was to remove from our walls at home all the photographs I had taken over the years and bring them in for Nancy to critique – which she did eagerly.

I asked her if she had a camera, and she did not. So I gave her mother a good camera that I no longer used, a way to assure that her strength would be nurtured, knowing that this was considered a violation of boundaries. It was breaking the rules, but nurturing the child's *island of strength*.

When she left, with her mother's encouragement I kept in touch. I took her on a guided nature photographic exploration at a nearby state park. I also arranged for her to shadow a photographer for the local daily newspaper and for her to spend time with a friend who does event photography. All violations of boundaries that spoke strongly in support of continuity of caring.

I was supposed to instead strike her from my memory when she was discharged from the facility. I was supposed to be one other person in her life who claimed to care, but only while getting paid. That's how she, and any other of my kids, would have interpreted it. (Sometimes when I got into trouble for acting responsively, I would keep my equilibrium by reciting George Orwell's quote: "If you clung to the truth even against the whole world, you were not mad.")

What is Nancy telling us . . . beyond her words?
For Nancy, the nurturing of her strengths and the help she later got through counseling at another facility served as the beginning of a new life. Nancy was a

wonderful example of how building on a child's island of strength can be accomplished by just a bit of ingenuity. By bringing in the local newspaper and an event photographer, Nancy was exposed to careers that built on her passion.

❋

Nobody, as long as he moves about among the chaotic currents of life, is without trouble.

-- Carl Jung

❋

CARLA

Carla's parents really cared about her, and she knew it. Still, when Carla's friends all decided to run away from home, she joined them.

They fled the small town where they lived and went to a large metropolis. There they entered the drug culture and, when their money ran out, they prostituted to keep their addictions fed.

One of the kids overdosed and died. This was a rude awakening for Carla (perhaps for the others as well), and she returned home. Her parents welcomed her back. No reprimand, just joy at her safe return. After all, she had already righted her wrong.

Around the time that this was happening, I was organizing a movement to establish a shelter for homeless youth. We got a good deal of publicity, including a feature article in the local daily newspaper. Carla saw the article and wrote to the paper, asking to be put in touch with the home's organizer. She wanted to help. And help she did. Carla's voice gave to our middle class, professionally littered experts, a reality base on which to build. It was Carla who would breech our fiscal conversations with questions like, "What will we do if a kid really just needs a hug?" Many times she knocked us off our tower of elitism, of book learning, and we landed gently in reality.

I lost contact with Carla and now, about ten years later, decided to try to find her. In this electronic age, it was not difficult, and I was successful. Carla is married now, and has a 7-year-old son. In between shuttling her son from swimming to acrobatics, she completed studies at a local college.

She is connected to her community through her volunteering, and her life is good.

What is Carla telling us . . . beyond her words?
Sometimes we all act impulsively, and it happens more frequently in our formative years. When a child "self-corrects," as when Carla did return home of her own volition, it is a time for celebration – not lecture or reprimand.

Carla kept the movement to establish a youth home on course. She gave us a reality base, having been briefly homeless herself and being the same age as the population we were to serve. We, as parents and counselors, must recognize the contributions young people can make. We do them (and ourselves) a great injustice if we devalue their thoughts and opinions. Carla is also presenting a strong argument for us to never give up on a struggling child, <u>never</u> to utter those oft spoken words, "That child will be in the system forever." It could have been said about her when she was drowning herself with drugs, selling her body, seeking out immediate gratification, and stressing her responsive parents. It could have been, but should not have been. I have heard those words spoken by co-workers too many times in my overlong life.

Give up on people, and you encourage their giving up on themselves.

✄

Heroin

the world swam before my eyes and i fall not being able
to catch myself,
but someone catches me though i cannot see them . . .
i feel them with every sense of the word . . .
i hear them breathing, and whispering to me
that it's going to be ok . . .
the last thought i have is am i going to die?
i awaken from a blissful state of unconsciousness
to abrupt pain all throughout my body,
it feels like i am being ripped apart
i itch at the needle marks on the inside of my elbow
and long for the numb feeling to come . . .
it doesn't . . .
and then you appear at my side.
you tell me that from now on you are my heroin
and that i would have died if you hadn't found me . . .
i tell you i love you and i cry . . .
there would be no more needles . . .

-- Mecanna Beah Karin
(pseudonym), A teen

73

JANE

Jane acted out all the time at home . . . and in detention. Her actions appeared to be erratic with no identifiable triggers to the behavior. In detention the attacks were directed toward other youth – most often verbal, but sometimes physical.

Jane, for all intents and purposes, never really had parents. She did live with the people who procreated and gave birth to her, but they lost all interest in her at birth (perhaps long before). There was no guidance provided to Jane, no fun times, no boundaries of behavior established.

One thing was clear: Jane had no control over her actions, let alone her attitude, and the punitive approach of the facility just made things worse.

We were sitting around in the living room one day when, for no apparent reason, Jane went off on another youth. The other child had been her antagonist since his arrival but until this event, Jane seemed to be tolerating him, making only an occasional derogatory remark.

This time was different.

Jane leaped up and, with her face in his space, physically threatened him. He ran into the dining room, jumped on the table and, brandishing a kitchen knife, threatened to kill her.

War had been declared between the two.

The supervisor stayed in her office, while I and another staff member separated them. When things had calmed, one member of the staff took the boy outside to shoot hoops, and I spoke to Jane.

There was no reason at this point to be concerned about safety, as the volatility of the event had been

74

neutralized. But perhaps this was an opportunity to help Jane gain insight about what had happened . . . and how it could have unfolded differently. I admit, though, that I wasn't optimistic.

We talked (as usual, mostly I listened), and Jane began a tirade about this evil boy and how despicable he was. I let her continue until she finally fizzled out. Then I introduced the possibility of alternative approaches of behavior when she felt that way. I was surely not going to challenge her feelings – to do so would have closed her off to help. Anyway, everyone's feelings are supported by their own claim to credibility, and challenges are, by definition, invalid.

One of the reasons I like working with adolescents is that there are so many surprises, so many unanticipated breakthroughs – many at unpredictable times. This proved to be one.

Jane seized on the opportunity to introspect (she had not previously demonstrated that ability), and started rambling about how she gets upset . . . does things she doesn't want to do . . . pays the price for it . . . hurts herself.

Then came a period of silence. Our society has grown so dependent on constant sound – be it radio, television, or conversation – we forget that silence is also a form of communication, too often excluded from our lives. Silence contributes to introspection, calmness, inner peace.

Jane was silent for some minutes. Then she looked at me, leaned forward, and said, "Mr. West, can you help me to not behave the way I do?"

I started to respond, but was cut off by the supervisor who emerged from her office. It might have been the silence that brought her out.

She started yelling at Jane that her behavior would not be tolerated under any circumstances. Jane's honest attempt to improve her life was collapsed by a few ill-spoken, shouted words.

We never again talked about her insights, her desire to move forward in her life, because she wouldn't allow it. She had opened up, displayed her vulnerability, but was shouted down by a higher authority. Her survival instincts were now on alert and she was closed-off to help.

What is Jane telling us . . . beyond her words? *Jane took a step toward self-awareness, and gave us a wonderful opportunity to walk with her in her quest. I was honored to be permitted to get close to her fears, life's frustrations, and uncertainty about how to control her emotions. A higher-level staff person perceived it as a vulnerability that needed to be addressed punitively.*

When a child has been so badly hurt in their vulnerable early childhood, when there is no one to reassure them and teach them how to accept love and guidance, that child takes on the responsibility of self-protection. An overwhelming burden for a young person.

Our society is blinded to the damage done by punishing and reprimanding those struggling.

Falling to Madness

I'm writhing on the edge of chaos,
descending slowly into madness,
it envelopes me in a warm comforting hug,
like a friend returned from long ago.
Splashes of imagery slammed into
where everything else was.

Warps to what is to be.
Losing days, weeks inside myself.
I'm not fully here I'm somewhere in the middle.
But I'm not fully there either.
Twisting in pain on the edge,
let go and lose myself,
or hold onto this weight.
As it crushes me slowly.

I force myself to kneel,
Stand and walk down my wavering line.
And smile.
All it took was courage.

All i need . . .
is courage.

-- Mecanna Beah Karin
(pseudonym), A teen

BETTINA

Her father meant well – love was his motivator – but he followed his daughter everywhere, and she felt suffocated. Her mother was silent to the oppressive "crowding" of the father to his children. Her older siblings had left home as soon as they were of age and never looked back. Bettina was the youngest. She ran, was caught, and sent to detention.

Every parent is tormented by the need to provide a wholesome expansive environment for their child, while simultaneously protecting them from the inherent dangers of life. Bettina's dad had trouble finding that comfortable balance, and his children suffered as a result. Still, no one could question his motivation – it was love of his children.

Bettina was an incredibly talented artist. On one occasion when I was planning to take the kids to the goat farm, I asked an artist friend of mine to meet us there and do an art project. She showed up arms laden with paints, brushes and palettes. We did interpretive paintings of the animals – goats, of course, but also llamas, turkeys, donkeys and horses. The artist was swept away by Bettina's talent.

Bettina's *island of strength* was clearly identified, but that wasn't enough. She needed a nurturing environment for it to flourish, which her home did not provide.

After a couple of weeks in detention, Bettina had "served her sentence" for running from home, and was discharged back home. No help was provided to her family.

I ran into Bettina months later at the local library. She came up to me with a quickened step and said, "Guess what, Mr. West, I am going to drop out of school, and go see the world." I talked to her about her great art talent, and how she could see the world later. I said that if she ran now, she would never see her talent flourish. Now, a couple of years later, I am "friended" with her.   She is living an awesome life, designs jewelry, and has healthy relationships. Bettina has everything that she deserves and, best of all, she did it on her own (with a bit of nurturing).

What is Bettina telling us . . . beyond her words? Children need a nurturing environment, to be encouraged to explore, to push the limits (in healthy ways) that we establish for them. This is especially true for teens who have one foot already in the adult world and bear the burden of all the anxieties that go with it.

Communication between parent and child, especially when the child is passing through the teen years, is critical . . . and often difficult. Yet, just like with Bettina's dad, many parents believe that it is the parental role to authoritatively set and enforce limits – enforce obedience. No compromise. No negotiation. "Do what I say, because I am your parent!"

As parents, we often think and react instinctively. We trust our innate judgment – often more than we should.

✻

When I lead parenting workshops, participants would often tell me of the stigma of their enrolling . . . their neighbors putting down their efforts to improve. "You are a great mom," they were told. "You don't need a class." Strange how they would be supportive if the same person was taking a class to improve their computer skills, or their photographic abilities. But not when they want to improve their relationship with their children.

✂

I know of a single mom who had a horrible day at work. Her co-worker was out sick, and she had to carry the burden for both workloads. Also, her boss was more than usually crotchety.

When she got home at the end of this nightmarish day, she noticed that her daughter had uncharacteristically thrown her book bag and coat on the couch. Mom blew up, sending her 14-year-old daughter crying to her room. She remembered what we talked about in class and waited until she was calm. Nothing good comes out of screaming matches, not for parent or child.

Then she went up to her daughter's room, knocked, and was invited in. They both sat on the bed, and mom explained what a horrible day she had. She apologized for "bringing it home," and suggested they go to the mall to eat and shop. Her daughter could do her homework when they got back.

They had a wonderful time, came home, her daughter did her homework and went to bed.

Later that night mom's sister called (who, incidentally, had no children). Mom told sis what had happened, and her sister said, "My sister, you are crazy. You apologized? Now you have given up control of your daughter forever."

"Control over your children," which is what Bettina's father tried to do, is a very different mindset from what

parenting should be. And, as Kara already told us, the capacity to apologize is the expression of human vulnerability and is always well received.

For a child preparing to take the scary journey to adulthood, the comfort of knowing that it is all right to make mistakes and acknowledge them, makes the journey a lot less intimidating. Striving toward a fulfilled life is a worthy goal, but having to pretend that you are at journey's end without having ever made a mistake is a nightmare.

✖

JASON

There were only a couple of times that I was actually fearful for my safety at detention, and this night was one of them. We had no youth, and I was chatting with my co-worker, Sara, one of only two counselors there, besides myself, who I thought really cared about the kids.

The phone rang, and it was a police officer who told us we were getting a court remand, male . . . violent episode in the community . . . gang affiliation . . . 13-years-old.

We decided what bedroom we would assign him to and waited. The police soon brought the child, handcuffed and in shackles, paperwork intact. He appeared calm and resigned to whatever was to come next. Draped across his left shoulder was a red bandanna – a symbol of gang affiliation.

As soon as the police left, the boy became violent. He began kicking the walls, spitting, and cursing. He refused to shower before bed time, a facility policy.

I was comforted that Sara was my shift partner, because she was close to fearless. Sara had wanted to be a police officer, but later decided to pursue a career that would permit her to have a more positive long-term impact on young people. She became a detention counselor and did have that positive influence on many of the youth.

The boy would not give up the bandanna and, because he was the only youth there, we let it slide. In a way, it was his security blanket – an affiliation that, while certainly destructive in connotation, for now gave him a needed sense of belonging.

Jason kicked at walls and looked like he was going to explode at any minute. Things were escalating, and this boy, who was small for his age, was ready to kill!

We fed him as he had not eaten since breakfast and were finally able to convince him to shower.

Then he went to bed. A short time later, Sara motioned for me to come upstairs and listen at his door.

I heard him sobbing uncontrollably.

The next day, the director berated us for letting him keep his bandanna. "You gave up all control over him! You should have called the police to have them remove it!"

Calling the police would have been an implied statement to Jason that we could not maintain control. Then when they left, we would be faced with a renewed power struggle with him.

What is Jason telling us . . . beyond his words?
Beyond Jason's bravado was a very scared little boy. So often, I have seen a facade of anger and aggression, as a means of self-protection – a way of masking fear.

By permitting him to keep his bandanna, we met Jason in the place he was and demonstrated the art of compromise. A more rigid approach would have precipitated greater rebellion from the youth.

We should be asking ourselves why this little boy needed the security of his gang to pull him through the experience of detention and help him survive. What is missing in the lives of these children? What can we give them that will negate the need for so strong a rebellion?

But our introspection must be in the context of also recognizing that some mild and appropriate rebellion is simply a part of growing up, a testament that the child is becoming an adult.

�֎

The Storm (that was me)

The storm rages on
fierce above my head
violent bursts of light
and the earth quakes beneath my feet
The pain of this storm
knowing that I am sitting alone again
in the rain I will weep
Can you tell
when the salt mixes with the water
and the tears turn to blood
would anyone miss me?

-- Mecanna Beah Karin
(pseudonym), A teen

✖

JUAN

He was a Hispanic boy who came from the most abusive background I had ever heard about. At a young age, his family would keep him chained in the basement for extended periods. He suffered horrific abuse.

It would have been hard, in the abstract, to believe he had a chance at a healthy life. But it was not "in the abstract" that I met Juan.

I am always looking for a deeper understanding of the connection between a youth's past, and how it impacts on their behavior years later. Most of the time, it is pretty easily deciphered – the more a child has suffered, the less support they have been given, the longer the road to a positive and fulfilling life.

For some of these kids, it is easy to understand why many staff members are quick to predict that a particular child will ". . . be in the system forever." The mental damage from their past appears irreversible. The scars are so deep as to seem beyond healing; they are a death knell. That mindset carries with it the inherent desire to spend more time with those deemed salvageable, and the child considered "beyond help" deteriorates further because of the lack of attention, the lack of caring.

Juan might have been that child, were it not for his incredible spirit, his determination to overcome all obstacles. He was positive, enthusiastic. When Barack Obama was nominated for the Presidency, Juan told me he hoped that he will win because "that would make my election as the first Hispanic President an easier campaign."

He moved on to a long-term residential facility, but continued to write for more than a year. Later he was approved for independent living – the youngest ever in the state. As of the publication of this book, he had not yet run for President.

What is Juan telling us . . . beyond his words? *There is strength and courage in these young people that can become their entry to a better life. While they often conceal it from those around them who they are suspicious of, the most intolerable conditions cannot extinguish that spark.*

For Juan, it was never even concealed. Why was this boy, who came from hell, able to visualize with such clarity his hopes and aspirations? Where did his strength and courage come from? Why was he even in the best of spirits on every visiting day, when he alone did not have visitors?

I do not understand it. Some would use his story as documentation of a genetic propensity for good or bad, strength or weakness, optimism or pessimism. Others might argue that there was an unidentified social influence on his life.

You choose. But, regardless of which you do choose, be sure to vote for him when he appears on the presidential ballot.

✂

MARSHA

Marsha said she had to talk to me. She had poured her heart out to me over a 3-week period, so I simply said, "always." But then she told me that this time it was different.

"Oh?"

"Well, Mr. West, I am going to tell you something, but I will only tell it to you if you promise to take it in a good way, and only if you promise not to say a word afterward."

My options at this point were limited. If I refused her contractual terms, I was sure that Marcia would clam up, and I would go into eternity wondering what it was about. So I agreed, and we went into the office.

"Mr. West," she began, "a lot of people in my life have said they were listening to me, but you were the first person to really *hear* me. And because of that, for the first time in my life, I think I will be all right."

Of course I was flattered and, as always, felt privileged to have been invited into her soul. But I was also wondering why the conversation needed those provisos . . . whether I had been too quick to give up my "right of rebuttal," why I had to commit to a vow of silence . . . .

"Uhh . . . uhh, Mr. West," I knew the mystery was about to unravel. "I think you have a girl gene in you!" She turned and ran out of the office, fearing that I might breech my vow of silence.

Sometimes the kids just made me laugh.

What is Marsha telling us . . . beyond her words? *There is a critical difference between listening and really hearing.*

When I ran the parenting program at the local YMCA and came in for evening classes, there was a pre-teen girl always there who would be waiting for her single mom to finish work and take her home. She was very overweight, looked down when she spoke, and had low self-esteem.

We would chat, and we got to know each other fairly well.

One evening – on a whim – I asked her if she wanted to speak to the class. "They're tired of hearing from me," I said. She responded, looking at the floor, that she would think about it.

The following week, I came in and she said she would do it. I gave her no parameters, other than for her to talk about what is important to a child. Of all the topics she could have chosen, here is what she said (while making direct eye contact with each parent, I should add), "Do you know what it feels like to come home and say to your mom, 'Mom, I have a problem and I've got to talk to you.' And you say, 'Okay, talk to me while I wash the dishes.' "

This girl was deeply offended by her having to fit into mom's schedule at a time of crisis. She knew the difference between listening and really hearing. The former is when you are distracted by something else you are doing simultaneously, the latter is when you sit face to face and really hear your child. She understood it, but her mom did not.

She left to go home, and the group talked about it. They laughed and felt embarrassed, admitting that they do it often. "I just don't have time," went the refrain.

I gently reprimanded them, arguing that the conversation would not have gone more than ten minutes and, that after a short period, they most likely would have heard from their child, "What's to eat?" The dishes could wait.

There is a dramatic difference between listening to your child incidental to doing something else, and sitting down, leaning forward, making eye contact, perhaps touching their hand . . . and really hearing what they are saying to you.

�֎

A critical component of listening – of really hearing – is that you do so from a posture of respect for what they are saying. I am reminded of an event that took place in my community a few years ago. There was a teenage boy who would fish at a dam just about every day after school. One day the boy returned from fishing and said to his dad that he sensed something strange about the dam, something he never felt before. His father dismissed it, saying, "The dam is strong, experts check on it."

The next day the dam broke, and the area downstream flooded. It wreaked havoc on many families.

I cannot help but wonder if the father's response would have been the same, if an adult had brought him the observation.

✖

LORI

At 16, Lori was pregnant, and there was no father in the picture. I've seen it before with all too many girls, but Lori was different than most.

"Mr. West, I did a stupid thing . . . I wasn't careful," she told me. "But I am going to have the baby, keep it, and be the best mom I can. Please, Mr. West, please . . . please . . . please . . . take me to the library so I can get books on babies."

I took her there more than once, and she read every book she could find, not only on prenatal care, but also on parenting. We talked a great deal about her readings, and even role-played parenting situations. (She told me that I was terrible at role-playing the child, but she thought that my cry was pretty good.)

In the school that the kids attended (a facade to meet state requirements that every child, even kids placed in detention, be schooled), she made charts of prenatal development and the teacher hung them on the wall.

Lori was even careful about her diet. "I'm not just eating for myself, you know," she told me. She rejected fat-rich foods and calorie-rich desserts. We read package ingredients together.

Lori had an intense sense of responsibility far beyond her young age, and I felt good about her future and that of her child. I also felt privileged to be a part of her self-initiated learning process about how to parent a child – with knowledge, love, structure and dedication. I was confident that years later, if her child made a mistake, Lori would be supportive and help her correct it. But the facility director saw it differently.

"Mr. West, you are to stop taking Lori to the library and getting her those books," she told me. You are encouraging her immorality!"

The director was religious and did not condone unmarried pregnancy.

What is Lori telling us . . . beyond her words?
Lori was ahead of most, and showed a deepening sense of maturity. She sought out book wisdom, and talked with those staff willing to listen. She was building a strong foundation for both herself and her soon-to-be born child.

It is counterproductive to berate a child who has made a mistake and wants to make amends. It is also immoral to impose one's own religious beliefs on *another, simply because they are a prisoner of the system you administer.*

People make mistakes and, indeed, with young people it is often the mistake of having unprotected sex. In many instances struggling young girls are lured by the magically powerful aspects of being a parent, for which they are not prepared. But in this case, Lori was asking for support and encouragement. She had charted a course for herself, and any honest analysis would show it was a clear and well-planned travail. She was also being responsive to her as yet unborn child. She was asking for permission to right her wrong. She was growing up.

Hope is a thing with feathers
That perches in the soul
And sings the tune without words
And never stops at all

-- Emily Dickinson

Ruminations on Damaged Systems

The systems that have critical impact on the healthy development of our children are failing them. And they are getting worse every day. Where in the past public schools were permitted the flexibility to design meaningful programs that encouraged the creative development of our children, today they are crushed by the pressures of fiscal survival. Detention programs (and the court system) have moved toward meeting the general population's wishes for more punitive approaches. Society as a whole is being told that they must sacrifice personal privacy (and the dignity that goes with it) in the name of national security. We are too quick to diagnose our young . . . too quick to medicate away their stresses because it is expedient.

We need to stop, take a deep breath, and do a deep analysis of what we are doing right . . . and what we are doing wrong.

The School System

There is an alarming trend to homogenize youth who attend our public schools. Schools are teaching to the test and, for fear of losing funding, they are eliminating subjects that are not federally mandated. All attention is placed on those subjects that are "measurable."

Subjects that are cast aside like useless litter, include creative subjects like art and music, and physical releases such as sports and recess. Not only are they outlets for creativity and energy release, they also teach life-long lessons of socialization.

In many instances, they also help youngsters identify their *island of strength*.

I once met a girl who was an incredible artist and musician. She attended a well-respected public high school, where she was doing poorly in math. The school made her drop music and art on the theory that she would have more time to devote to her math studies. Instead she suffered an emotional collapse. They had removed her "islands of strength," and there was nothing positive left for her. Fortunately her parents took charge and enrolled her in a small responsive school, where she took math, music and art, and excelled in all three.

With struggling youth, this approach – this crushing of free spirit, this stripping away of the child's strengths and means of individual self-expression – is devastating for a number of reasons. Many of these kids are barely holding on to a frail reality, which is rife with stress. Yet they are being told to relinquish the few healthy means of expression that they have available to them. Their socialization skills are often poor, and by losing access to these expressive arenas they lose a comfortable place to interact with their peers and learn to relate in positive ways.

As a consequence, their behavior worsens and, to keep them from acting out, we demand compliance through punitive measures, or the administration of psychotropic medication. They rebel against the senseless punishments, and become enslaved to the power of the drugs. If they can't cope with the pressure of school and truant, we punish them by locking them up in detention.

The school system demands that kids be lumped together and required to fit into one mold, sacrificing individuality in the name of expeditious learning. It's essential to preserving the funding stream, we are told. Troubled youth get lost in the race, act out, become truant, and turn to drugs and alcohol. Classes are too large for the teacher to be able to identify (and work with) a struggling child. The kids are swallowed up by the system and get lost in the herd. Then we turn to diagnosing and medicating them, so that they will fit the mold.

As we depart from "no child left behind" to initiate "race to the top" (it has often been argued that education should be a journey, not a race), we denude our children's creativity, their curiosity, their individual personalities, their strengths . . . and crush them under a massive unwieldy structure.

In New York State, the Office of Children and Family Services (OCFS) posted a report on their website, entitled: "Getting Teenagers Back to School." They cite the disturbing statistic that, in the school year 2008-2009, 40% of students in the public school system were absent more than 20 days.

In this ten-page policy brief, the agency candidly admits to being ill-equipped to deal with the truancy problem. But they are undermining their own potential influence. Really, it is not that complicated, as demonstrated by a number of schools that have successfully drawn their students back. However, it does carry the prerequisite of being able to think outside the box, and not place the entire burden on the children and their parents. Put excitement back in the curriculum, give kids avenues for self-expression, reach out and provide guidance to parents . . . and, most importantly, provide opportunities for kids to learn skills that nurture their passions. Do that, and attendance will rise.

OCFS needs to partner with their local school system, because the frightening problems we face today cross agency lines. We are all in this struggle together . . . or at least we should be.

Watch the movie *Freedom Writers* to see how the system can be made more responsive; read the bibliography at the back of this book for more; read about the Missouri system. It's all been done before.

Our efforts will not be successful unless we can step back, take a hard look at our own failings, *and listen to our kids*. But for them to talk freely, comfortably, they have first got to trust us. It starts with our being honest and expressing genuine caring. The rigid bureaucratic attitudes that you read about in some of the stories is exactly what closes kids off and makes them distrustful. If we want them to adapt to the needs of the school system, we will only be successful if we first demonstrate that the system can be adapted to their needs – each child, individually. "Homogenization" of the kids is toxic to the process!

❀

In New York State, chronic unexplained absenteeism can bring charges of child neglect against the parent. The requirement to investigate overtaxes the same agency that is also mandated to protect children from abuse. These departments have already suffered the effects of budget cuts, and now they are diverted from the critical task of protecting children by an arbitrary rule to punish parents without considering the circumstances.

Is our being so punitive a product of our own insecurity? Why are we so resistant to overhauling systems that are failing? Don't we recognize these failings, at least in part, as being our own responsibility? Accepting our vulnerability, our failures, and taking corrective action is a sign of strength. We have admiration for people in the public eye who have done it. We need to do it.

✄

Cleveland recently passed a law that if a parent misses two school meetings, they are subject to arrest. This is another example of how government addresses problems punitively, instead of responsively. Working with parents, giving them the parenting skills they lack, is far more effective than punishing them. What if a poor family could not get transportation, or if they had other children and could not afford a babysitter? Perhaps they had a sick child in need of care.

Are the arrested parents, who are often poverty stricken, charged a fine? Or are they put in jail? What effect do we think jailing parents has on the emotional stability of their kids?

Why are we so punitive?

✄

BREAKING THE RULES

I have been judging 4-H Public Presentations for many years. The kids work on picking a subject of interest, write their presentation, practice it before their peers (who act as judges), until finally the day comes when they present it before "real" judges like myself. They are both nervous and excited. Teachers have told us that in a new class they can spot the kids who have been in 4-H by how their approach to problem solving is more organized, more logical.

When one particular night of judging had ended, I was hit with the realization that all six of the kids I judged seemed to be unusually calm and more accepting of my critiques than other youngsters had been in the past. In fact, a couple of the kids even asked for elaborations on my suggested points of improvement.

Speaking to their parents later, I learned that all six kids had been home-schooled.

How much of the philosophy of home-schooling can be incorporated into the public school system?

If a home-schooled child is having a stressed day (or if their teaching parent is), they can work around it; a home-schooling curriculum nurtures a child's special interests; testing of home-schooled children is only a secondary means of measuring what they learned; there is no teaching to the test because there is no funding component. Most important is that when it is done right, the child is enveloped in a cocoon of comfort, an environment that makes them eager to learn. And the information stays with them because they are not learning just to demonstrate their knowledge on a test.

A baby is born with natural curiosity. As soon as they are able, they will touch, taste and explore any object within reach. Their world expands as they learn to crawl, then again when they can walk (and, as many a parent will attest, also run).

While this is happening, their cognitive abilities are being enhanced, and their own personalities are being refined. They grow comfortable in themselves. Some infants and children soon learn that they are good climbers, others are more artistic. Some are active, others pensive. The astute parent, right from this early age, will nurture their child's strengths. This builds self-confidence, but it can only happen if the child is recognized for their individuality – their uniqueness.

It doesn't happen in the school system, where they are shoved into categories, required to adapt to the teaching regimen, forced to give up their uniqueness so as to conform to a norm. Some are able to do it more easily than others. Some are destroyed trying.

So how much of the home-schooling practices can be applied to the public school system? I don't know. But I do know two things: that if we don't try, we will never have the answer, and that our public schools are failing our kids.

As we leave "no child left behind," and initiate "race to the top," we extract that child's creativity, their curiosity, their individual personalities, their strengths, and replace them with a massive structure that demands they conform, and that they learn for the sake of the test.

✿

Educating Kids in Detention

By law, kids in detention must continue their education while in confinement. But, as with so many other mandates intended to protect these kids, there is no reality base to the implementation.

There are two distinct approaches a detention facility can take to meet their education mandate.

Some facilities send their kids to the district public school in which the facility is located. In those instances, children who already have weak socialization skills and are behind in their studies, now find themselves in a new setting, with unfamiliar teachers (and students), and an alien curriculum. They also are an easy target of harassment from the "regular" student body. All of this makes for an unsettling environment, which leads to unstable reactions.

Remember that these kids were not coping even before this abrupt change. We set them up for another failure!

Other facilities have gone the route of maintaining their own internal school structure. This permits smaller classes and, theoretically, employing teachers who are skilled at working with this population. Most important is that the programs can be adapted to the individual needs of each youngster. (Funding is not dependent on performance in this setting.) If done well, it can be an excellent step toward infusing some of the benefits derived by home-schooling. If done poorly, it is another failure with which the kids will have to try to cope.

Where I worked, we did in-house education and we did it poorly! The teacher was assigned by the local school principal, and the class was comprised only of our detention kids. So what teacher would the school principal assign to these "cast out" kids? Surely not one of her strongest motivators . . . the teacher who generates high test scores . . . the one who helps to preserve the funding stream in their base school. No, indeed. We were assigned a teacher who was ill-suited to teach a regular curriculum and, by definition, even less suited to teach struggling youngsters. He was often even afraid of some of the kids, and they knew it.

I do not believe this teacher felt any enthusiasm for teaching, so how could the kids for learning? He frequently showed DVDs, played games, and never came in with a lesson plan. In fairness, it must be said that this was a short-term facility and, although he did comply with the requirement that he request their school work from their regular public school, it often was not sent (because these are throwaway kids so why waste the time), or it arrived after they had been transferred or discharged.

One time he did come in with an elaborate presentation about the civil rights movement. He opened with a PowerPoint presentation of the Jefferson Memorial, explaining that this was the site of many civil rights demonstrations, including Martin Luther King's famous speech, "I Have a Dream." I had to explain to him that it was the Lincoln Memorial, Jefferson was a major slave holder, and that would have been a poor choice of location for a civil rights demonstration! I was, however, impressed with his effort . . . the work he did to try to make his presentation meaningful, even exciting. At least he tried.

In the early stages of my employment there, school was held in a rented classroom off-site from the detention facility. It was also an all-day program, with a break for lunch. This symbolically gave it some respectability. Later, the sponsoring school cut the classes to half a day, and no longer rented space elsewhere. So the kids had to try to learn at the detention facility's dining room table, with many interruptions. We showed no respect for their education, so neither did they.

What could have been accomplished in the short time a child was there? In addition to working on improving their knowledge in the subjects where they were weak (a phone call to their school guidance counselor might have been a better way to obtain that information), they could have been turned on to learning about fields that interested them. What an opportunity: a class with a maximum of six students and with a counselor to help.

We could have sent them out with a thirst for more knowledge and possibly visions of a career. Instead, all we did was comply with a state mandate to provide a certain number of hours of education. Glorified babysitting at best!

In reality, it would have been better if I had been given the opportunity to take them to more museums, go on more hikes, or visit places that would fuel their passions, their islands of strength.

Discipline is Different from Punishment

In fact the root of the word "discipline" is disciple – meaning teacher or, to teach.

At the detention facility where I was employed, disciplinary action – substitute the word punishment – regardless of offense, was to have the child repetitively write that they will not commit that offense again. It was called a target skill, a misnomer if ever there was one.

Here is how it worked. A child who curses at another child, for example, would have to write 20 times that they will not curse at that child again. For many of these youngsters, writing was a healthy release of tension. They wrote poetry, kept journals, wrote original music, short stories. We turned it punitive!

This punishment would often enrage the kids, and they would refuse to cooperate. As a result, they lost privileges, like participating in sports, which was a release of tension for them. If the other youth were watching television, this child would have to remove himself to another room, or turn his back to the T.V. (If something exciting happened in the program, and he reflexibly turned toward the television, he was reprimanded.)

The offender grew bored, angry, and got restless as a result of the restrictions. Finally, if he still refused the writing assignment, it was not pursued, teaching all the wrong lessons about compliance.

My boss once complained to me that I don't give the kids disciplinary write-ups often enough. I explained that they don't act out with me (something she already knew), and she replied, "You need to find a reason to write them up, because you're making other staff look bad."

❊

In the home lives of so many of these kids, boundaries were either lacking or enforced to excess. Parents who physically assaulted their children were as commonplace as those who ignored them. The opportunity for positive dialogue was often non-existent in their homes, and they never learned the art of negotiation, compromise, and acceptance. Family-sharing activities were an unfulfilled dream for many of these desperate children. To provide what they were lacking in terms of self-esteem, communicative skills, and social skills takes planning and patience. It cannot be pieced together in a quilt of punishment when they misstep; it has to be designed around a core of respect. And it certainly should not tread on something positive in their lives . . . a healthy means of expression.

✄

Privacy Goes with Respect

The children at my place of employment were given journals and told it would be for their eyes only. But they were not permitted to take the journals upstairs to bed with them, and staff read them when the children were asleep. Some had a hunch that the reason for the restriction was to invade their privacy. Others simply wondered why, at a really expressive time for them just before bed, they were not permitted to free themselves of the burdens of the day by writing.

I never invaded their privacy. This is not a foundation for respect – the base on which to build trust. It fuels the suspicion that these kids already have. (Of course, if I were to lose their trust, they most likely would have acted out with me, which would have provided me with opportunities to write them up, satisfying my boss.)

The kids were not permitted to engage in private conversations for fear that they would pass subversive information. There were "target skills" given for whispering, or even talking in a normal tone out of earshot of a counselor.

Idle Time Weighs Heavy for Kids in Detention

They are often there with kids they did not know before and do not like. It is sometimes worse when they know the kids – they form cliques to the exclusion of other kids, and tell war stories to each other, glorifying their misdeeds.

Getting them out of the facility had many positive attributes, beyond just the avoidance of confrontation. It exposed them to new worlds (what an opportunity for them to identify their islands of strength), and taught social skills and appropriate public behavior.

One of my favorite outings was to a local museum that is really the old house of a deceased wealthy woman. On the way down, the kids would ask me where we were going, and when I said to a museum, the response most often heard was, "I don't want to go to no museum, Mr. West."

I ignored their protestations, because I knew what was to come.

In the vestibule of this museum was a larger than life bronze statue of a woman holding four flowers in one hand with the other arm outstretched and pointing to the sky. As my apathetic group entered, we stopped at the statue. "Hey, guys, what is going on in this woman's life," I asked. A few lethargic responses were all I usually got.

I knew the history of the pieces because my wife had worked there as a volunteer docent. "This statue had actually been on a grave, and was stolen," I explained. Now I had their interest, thanks to my careful infusion of the word "stolen" in the dialogue. Some postulated that the woman was pointing to heaven, and I added that the flowers were for her four children.

We lumbered on.

In the house, they would invariably stop at the first piece and ask about it. I would respond, "No, no, no, there is something I am dying to show you first. (It was true . . . I was excited to, well . . . get them excited. Excitement is contagious.)

We moved into what was the dining room, now at a quickened pace, stopping in front of a dark painting of a young woman with a sour expression. Dark clothes, dark background, dark expression on her face.

"What's going on here?"

"Well, Mr. West, I think she's pissed . . . oops, I mean mad."

"Any others?"

"Yea, everything is so dark that it's sad."

"Good insights, my children." I said, recognizing that I was using a term of endearment and breaking the rules. "In fact she *was* angry, and it *is* a depressing scene. The girl's father was the artist, and he was crazy (I had them hooked now . . . "stolen" and "crazy" in one outing . . . they were totally sucked in). He made her go out into the woods to live for weeks at a time, with no food at all.

There was no need to excite them about any other pieces – the excitement came from within. "Mr. West, why are their beds so small?" "Hey, isn't there another painting behind this one?" "How did she get rich?" "What is this painting about?"

Their minds had come alive!

We always stopped at the gift shop on the way out, and I bought each a small gift. Most chose a postcard of a painting they liked, or a scene of the museum. A token of a good memory and my wishes that there would be many more. I got some pretty amazed looks from new kids who couldn't (yet) understand why someone who was a paid employee would care enough to give them a gift.

On the way home, I predictably heard the same question. "Mr. West, is there another museum we can go to tomorrow?"

We didn't only go to museums. We went in hunt of garnets at a mine that was open to the public . . . we went on hikes . . . we did snowshoeing . . . animal tracking . . . we made giant snow murals, and built snowmen and snowwomen. We opened up new vistas that, with the right support, could later be nurtured into careers. And we talked, questioned, debated about everything. They challenged me, respectfully (and comfortably). I often thought that this skill might have been the most important that I nurtured in them.

I also wanted to take individual kids to places that were related to their particular interests . . . their passions. For example, I wanted to take Elinor, the girl with the tremendous potential to become a chef, to visit the kitchen of a well-respected restaurant that friends owned. The director said that would be favoritism, and refused my request. She was unable to differentiate individual attention and support, from favoritism. I would have taken any child to any place that would fuel their passions, and make their future seem more attainable.

Small Gestures Send Strong Messages

For example, how should youth address staff? Most facilities have them use the staff member's first name. (They do not give the last name for fear of later retaliation from the youth.)

The place I worked had a unique approach (as was too often the case). Staff would use the first letter of their last name and be addressed, Mr. B., or Ms. T. With so many changes in staff as shifts changed, and the high staff turnover generally, it was extremely confusing to the youngsters. It was unreal!

Fortunately, we had so many "W's" on staff that I was given permission to use my full last name. I was addressed as Mr. West and never suffered retaliation. The kids and I respected each other too much for that to happen. In fact, I may have been the only counselor in the facility that had a listed home telephone number.

Small, seemingly meaningless rules were imposed to protect from certain contingencies that rarely (more often never) occurred. They made the kids feel less relaxed, more uptight, and closed them off to the help they desperately needed.

Some examples: Singing or dancing was not permitted. "They may send gang signals!" Music is especially important to teens, it is a form of camaraderie, of bonding, of sharing. So how often did they send gang signals through music before it was banned? Actually, to the best of my knowledge, it had never happened!

Children were not permitted to go to the bathroom within 2 hours of a meal. One supervisor told me not to divulge the reason, because ". . . they need to learn how to follow rules." What was the reason for the rule? It was the concern that a child might be anorexic, and would go in and purge themselves of the meal. How often had it happened? Actually there were no cases in which there was documentation it ever happened there.

Ironically, because that rule led to so much resistance, it was modified. If you really had to go you could, but only if you sang (or spoke) the entire time. I guess the director felt that a child would not demean their gang by sending "singing gang signals" from a bathroom.

In each of these cases, the child was being treated as suspect, even though there was no evidence at all that what they did, or intended to do, was to violate any rules. How would you feel? How would you react? The kids reacted with tension in their body, anger in their heart.

�֎

I know of a school principal who is a staunch supporter of the philosophy that no exception to any rule is justified. If kids are walking down the hall with their hat on, this principal will single out the most volatile child for punishment. The child usually rebels, and the principal orders in-school detention. It is the same school that Athena attended . . . the school where she was held captive in the room she had fled to for sanctuary.

✖

At the detention facility, there was a chore chart hanging in the kitchen. After meals, each child would look up their bed number on the chart, then slide their finger over to the correct day of the week, and the meal just completed (breakfast, lunch, dinner). That would reveal their chore. It was a functional system.

On weekends, I was there without the director being present. So often, instead of reverting to the chore chart, when the meal was completed I simply said something like, "okay guys, let's clean up." The effect of treating them with this new-found sense of respect and responsibility was heartwarming. I wish I had filmed it. The kids all pitched in, each helping the other. Chores got done quicker, and more efficiently. Often said to a new youth from a peer were things like, "just a second Josh, and I'll give you a hand with that, as soon as I finish what I am doing."

Oh, the power of feeling respected, trusted to do the right thing!

❁

I always arrived about a half hour or more before the beginning of my shift. I used that time to socialize with the kids, joke and challenge them. (Whenever I returned from a day off, they would give me a big hello when I walked in. I would stop them, and say, "Don't give me a hello unless you first tell me, what is the only vegetable you cannot buy frozen, processed or canned" – or pose a similar challenge.) We would talk and joke and, when my shift formally began, I would casually swipe my time card. The kids recognized that my coming early and spending time with them off the clock can only be interpreted as caring about them. They were perceptive.

To swipe your card, signifying to kids that you are

now on the clock, then tell them you care, is not credible.

✄

When kids were putting each other down, I would sometimes pull out what I called my "Native American Naming Game." But only if the kids had not passed over the line beyond which they could not laugh at themselves and recognize the absurdity of some of their attitudes. In other words, I could not use it often.

Here is how it worked.

I would explain to the kids that Native Americans name their children based on their strong qualities. So a tall person might be called, "Boy who Walks on Tree Tops." A fast runner might be, "Girl who Runs with the Wolves."

Then we would go around naming every child in the group, having to search for their strong, positive qualities. Some that I recall emerging, names given to a peer who a few minutes ago was an adversary, included:

"Boy with the Wicked Jump Shot," "Girl who has Read Every Book," "Girl who Draws like Walt Disney," "Boy who Keeps Anger in his Back Pocket."

With the light frivolity of a game, kids were subtly led to a better place – one where every person had strengths and virtues not formerly recognized.

By no means was it a permanent "fix." But it was meeting the children where they were, and introducing alternative possibilities.

✄

Staffing a Detention Facility – The Damage Done When You Do It Wrong

A friend of mine who runs an incredibly responsive home for detention youth was telling me recently about their orientation program. It was creative, challenging, and really prepared a new staff member to be effective right from the start.

Where I worked, orientation consisted of reading large patchwork books, then signing off on each. While there were opportunities to ask questions, there was no planned discussion. Worse, as you read, it started to sound familiar and you realized that you had read those exact pages in another book, perhaps the day before. We used to watch for a look of recognition, of familiarity on the faces of new recruits as they plundered through the books.

In the responsive facility I mentioned, not only was the preparation meaningful for the new employee, but the supervisory staff was also afforded the opportunity to gauge the competence and commitment of each new staff person – before they had any extensive interaction with the kids. Why is that so important? Let me tell you of a consequence of not having that . . . of something that went terribly wrong where I worked.

Soon after I began work at detention, an employee was hired who had a degree from a state university. We'll call him Frankie. He immediately established that he was not interested in the kids, would watch sports on television, and read most of the time. He interacted with the kids only when he desired, or when they were

110

acting out. One youth wrote on her exit interview that someone should tell this employee not to spend his shift texting friends. She elaborated that it was clear that he was only there for the paycheck.

When he invited youth outside to shoot hoops, he picked the kids with whom he wanted to play. He would take them to the YMCA because he enjoyed participatory sports, but rarely anywhere else.

When a girl said to him that her life was over and she might as well end it, he said casually, "go ahead."

One evening, two girls were having a conversation about the ethnic origin of various hair styles. Whenever this happened, I would lay back and listen, not wanting to interrupt the healthy flow of dialogue between them. One girl said to the other that Afros are obviously of African origin but, she asked, "Aren't dreads Caribbean?" Before the other girl could respond, Frankie called out from another room, "Dreads are dirty and the people who wear them are dirty. All they do is remind me of chicken and grits."

The girls abruptly ended the conversation, and turned on the television.

When Brittany returned to us (we already heard from her), he said to her, "I would have thought you would have gotten it right by now." He made no claims toward empathy, having come from a privileged life himself.

I complained to a supervisor almost daily about his attitude and behavior, but he was the model counselor at the facility as seen from the distorted eyes of the director. He was revered, as much as I was held in contempt.

On a stormy night, we received notification from the main office that non-essential personnel may leave early. Since there was only one child there, a girl, I and another co-worker left. Frankie said he needed the money and would stay on. He was alone with the 14-year-old girl!

He had sex with her, statutory rape by an employee with a girl half his age. We learned about it many months later when she divulged what had happened to a counselor at a drug rehabilitation facility. Frankie was arrested, pled guilty and, as I write, is serving time in prison.

The exemplary employee had dropped in status!

He would never have survived the orientation at this other facility. He would have been seen for who he was, and dismissed (if, in fact, he was ever hired).

Why was someone who saw the kids as a commodity permitted to work with this highly vulnerable population? Why was he the apple of the director's eye? Isn't it clear that if you respect the children, you will not defame them?

Testing – It can be a Tool or a Weapon of Mass Destruction

There was a time when we labeled dyslexic children as stupid, visually or hearing impaired as lazy. With testing came the ability to identify basic problems and provide targeted help.

Then, as we are prone to do, we took it to an unhealthy extreme. Today, a child with an abundance of energy (formally considered a good quality) is, these days, tested and found to suffer from ADHD; a young person who, as we all have, suffered a period of uncertainty and depression is tested and found to suffer chronic depression; a two-year-old, smitten with his new-found mobility who objects to any restrictions placed on him, is diagnosed as oppositional; an adolescent who is testing the waters of adult life . . . pushing the limits of their youth, is found to be suffering from Oppositional Defiance Disorder.

And for each there is a pill.

Parents have the right to refuse psychological testing for their child but that option is often either not presented, or it is minimized by creating an atmosphere of fear as to what would happen if a problem were missed. When testing is done, and a diagnosis rendered, the option of getting a second opinion is almost never presented.

Good parenting must include periodically getting a copy of your child's records. All of them – from teachers notes, to psychological evaluations (you would be surprised how often parents were not even informed that the tests were done), to disciplinary actions. All records! You have the legal right to them, something most schools are not quick to inform you about.

Isn't it curious how identifying a diagnosis so often parallels available funding? In one school district, when funding became available for special help for ADHD identified students, the number of kids diagnosed through testing as having ADHD in that district instantly jumped by 35%!

Psychological testing implies objectivity, but does not account for so many variables. An attorney friend once said to me, "give me a diagnosis you want for a youngster, and I will tell you which practitioner you should go to for testing." We often find what we are looking for.

My son once received a conceptual test. They showed him a picture and asked him to find a list of hidden items. He couldn't find any and they decided that he had conceptual problems. (I don't think they had a pill for that at the time.)

I asked to show it to him, and I said, "You don't see the jug, the bird, and so forth?" He said, "Sure I do. Here's the jug, the bird . . . ." He found every item. When I asked him why he didn't point them out to the tester, he explained, "They aren't hidden. She said to find hidden ones."

Testing is fueled by the need to find pathology as a precursor to treatment. Many of the tests, and the testers, bring with them both a racial and cultural bias. Pathology is found much more frequently among minorities, because that is where the tester looks harder for it. Again, we find what we are looking for.

In one court case, a psychologist who evaluated the drawings of two girls, one 4- and the other 5-years-old, cited these criteria for evidence of pathology:
- Shapes that are untypical for 3- and 4-year-old children
- Shapes that are phallic symbols
- Jiggly lines that indicate anxiety
- Straight mouths that mean people can't say anything
- Jagged mouths that mean anxiety
- A mouth that is open and oval shaped
- Darkened eyes
- Eyeballs that are scribbled around
- Eyes that are two different colors

- Drawing something and then covering it up
- Drawing something and not talking about it

"Colors are very important and significant," she said. "The use of black means the child is frightened or distressed, because it is a morbid, down color; red means angry, unless the child is drawing a pretty red flower; if everything in the picture is red or red and black, this is very suspicious; blue, brown, and orange mean fear, anger."

It is enough to make you never want to pick up a crayon again!

(For more examples of erroneous clinical interpretations of children's art, go to: www.ipt-forensics.com/library/images5.htm.)

Would you want your child evaluated against these rigid criteria? Can you imagine the damage that this can do to a struggling youth and his family . . . the pathology identified, the medication prescribed?

If drawing a straight mouth, or a jagged mouth, or a mouth that is open and oval shaped is all symptomatic, what shape of mouth is evidence of the artist's emotional stability?

I know a girl who has one blue eye, and the other green. She used to be embarrassed, until her father explained that she was unique in her school . . . special. Then she was proud. But if she did a self-portrait, would she be risking a diagnosis?

❉

A 4-year-old girl who lived in Texas was asked to draw a tree, which she did. However, she also included a cactus plant in her drawing. The therapist interpreted this as ". . . an unconscious expression of danger and

115

fearfulness." Perhaps the child simply had a cactus growing in her backyard. After all, she lived in Texas!

✄

A psychologist rolled a multi-colored inflated ball to a 6-year-old boy. He picked it up and turned it in his hands. The psychologist determined that this was evidence of disturbance because "he should have rolled the ball back." So much for a child's curiosity, for their creativity.

✄

A method to identify *potentially* violent children, "Mosaic 2000," was utilized without parental consent or awareness in a number of schools. It was tested in random schools across the country and may prove to be a precursor for criminal profiling of our youth. Imagine what they will find from testing in the schools our detention youth attend.

The testing agency has repeatedly refused to disclose the questions asked on the test.

✄

A program created by Columbia University, TeenScreen, followed on the heels of a Presidential Commission recommendation that every teen in the United States be screened (substitute the word tested) for signs of *potential* mental illness and that they receive treatment where indicated. Millions of dollars were poured into this national effort. What's wrong with trying to identify potentially troubled youth? It can't be done. There is no valid test that can objectively identify a propensity toward emotional illness (Horwitz & Wakefield, 2009).

The program only utilizes a brief questionnaire and, if certain items are checked, it flags that response. Here are some sample questions:

- *Has there been a time when nothing was fun for you and you just weren't interested in anything?*
- *Has there been a time when you felt you couldn't do anything well or that you weren't as good-looking or as smart as other people?*
- *How often did your parents get annoyed or upset with you because of the way you were feeling or acting?*

TeenScreen is heavily-laden with false positives. Large numbers of youth are mistakenly identified as potentially mentally ill.

Such instruments indicate that about a third of adolescents have, or are at risk for, depressive disorders. One study of the TeenScreen instrument identified from 28% to 44% of all the students as having the potential for suicide (Horwitz and Wakefield 2009). The study concluded, in part: "This may reflect the pathologizing of *normal sadness* which results from stressful events in young lives" (this author's italics).

It is ironic that, in these times, it is the schools that are so often the major stress generators in the lives of our young people.

Why do youth participate in the testing, and why do parents consent? TeenScreen approaches the child first, offering incentives like free movie passes. Once the child is hooked, they go to the parents for consent.

117

There have also been allegations that sometimes they test without parental consent.

Current epidemiological information suggests that depression occurs in approximately 4% to 8% of adolescents (Larcada 2007), a dramatically lower number than is identified through TeenScreen (although they are quick to preface their findings with the word "potential"). Of course, regardless of the terminology, once the child is labeled they often begin a long journey of legal drug enslavement.

✄

Mental Diagnosis – An Often Abused Tool

The Diagnostic and Statistical Manual of Mental Disorders (DSM) is a publication of the American Psychiatric Association and is an attempt to standardize mental diagnoses. It is controversial and, at best, the beginning of a categorization process that denudes any attempt at treating the patient as unique and providing meaningful help.

The presumed-to-be-accurate diagnosis is the precursor to a pigeonholing approach to treatment, which is based on the concept that all that is needed to "cure" is to eliminate the "disease," whether through therapy, medication, or a combination of both. However, even when that goal is achieved, the individual is left with a void, because nothing positive had been incorporated into their life – only a negative (the pathology) removed.

A newer and more positive approach is to build on the positive aspects of the child's being. You read about that as you met my kids, and you witnessed the metamorphosis for many of them. They discovered their healthy inner selves, and their problems dissolved. Not overnight, but in its own time.

What we might well label the "Pathological Diagnosis and Exorcism Approach" is still favored by the majority of conventional practitioners and continues to dominate the field. And the DSM is the commander of the troops.

Consider that the rates for diagnosing pediatric bipolar disorder has witnessed an increase of 4,000% between 1994 and 2003, where the increase for diagnosing adults with the same disorder only rose by approximately 180 percent (Sharp & Hellings, 2006).

On average, 11 million prescriptions for anti-depressants for adolescents alone are written every year in the United States. And no age is immune. There is an alarming trend to prescribe these drugs for younger and younger children. A Columbia University study recently found a doubling of the rate of prescribing anti-psychotic drugs for privately insured *2- to 5-year-olds* from 2000 to 2007 (*APA Working Group*).

In our search for pathology, we become blind to our children's strengths. Then we obfuscate those strengths with chemicals, in the name of eliminating the pathology. It is ironic because, ultimately, it is their strength and courage that, if nurtured, breaks through and helps these youngsters survive . . . and thrive.

Listening as an Alternative to Condemning: The Juggalos – A Case Study

They are growing in numbers across the country and are followers of Insane Clown Posse – a musical group with a rebellious attitude. There have been a few instances where a horrific assault was perpetrated on a teen and investigations revealed that the perpetrator was a follower of the Juggalos. None of these attacks have ever been linked to a Juggalo philosophy or approved practice. It would be no less erroneous to highlight that an aggressor was Catholic, Protestant, Jewish, a carpenter or seamstress.

Their conversations are laced with expletives that would shock even the most sophisticated adult.

Rebellious cursing teens . . . a reason to condemn them, right? But wait. Let's look beyond the lyrics . . . beyond their words.

They just completed a charity Christmas toy drive for kids who would otherwise go without. Granted, their web casts soliciting toys were riddled with their trademark obscenities, one ending with, "Thank you for giving a f-ck." Still, looking beyond the words, can it be construed as anything less than an attempt to be *connected to community?*

Their frequently chanted slogan is, "We will not die alone." This provides further insights into their deeper motivations, the reason for forming such a strong bond with each other . . . their sense of how society has ostracized them in the past. One Juggalo, in an interview, said, "It's about family, because we are considered outcasts."

One of their websites (they have "chapters" throughout the country, most with their own website), lists famous people who, in their teens, were Juggalos. Many of them would surprise you. Another says, "People should be known for who they are and who they choose to be, not by whom they so choose to listen to [a reference to their music]."

There is much controversy about whether the Juggalos meet the criteria to be considered a gang, and a number of their websites address this directly. One states, "If you look at the criteria that the cops give to be considered gang related, then you would see that the cops themselves would be considered a gang. There's more than three of them, they all have a common sign (badges), and they all wear the same uniforms in their respective cities."

Another states, "They consider us a gang but if you use the reasons they post [about our] group of people same ideals, symbols, etc., most every religion [could be considered] of being gang related."

I don't know whether the Juggalos warrant a gang classification, and our apparent preoccupation with it might even be evidence of our attempt to satisfy our own need to pigeon-hole, to homogenize them into a broad-sweeping category. I do know that the Juggalos, to use a business term, have found their market. They are in great demand.

It's difficult to estimate the total number of Juggalos, but a 2009 gathering brought out 20,000 people. Even more dramatic is that the most recent Insane Clown Posse album, which received *no* commercial media coverage, still sold about 50,000 copies *in the first week of release.*

I ask again: What are we not giving these youngsters that make them fear dying alone? Why do they need to protect themselves from being further ostracized by society? Why do we care about their music, conveniently ignoring the groups that we followed obsessively in our own youth? And how important is the way they dress? Finally, what good purpose is served by our distorting an aggressive incident so that it appears it was not the result of a deranged person but, instead, represents the Juggalos as a group?

We are not evil. We don't harm or seduce people.
We are not dangerous. We are ordinary people like you.
We have families, jobs, hopes, and dreams.
We are not a cult.
This religion is not a joke.
We are not what you think we are from looking at T.V.
We are real. We laugh, we cry. We are serious.
We have a sense of humor.
You don't have to be afraid of us.
We don't want to convert you.
And please don't try to convert us.
Just give us the same right we give you
--to live in peace.
We are much more similar to you than you think.

-- Margot Adler,
Wiccan priestess

Government Policies do not Always Make Sense

Recently I read a study to determine whether, when siblings are placed in foster care, they do better if placed in the same home. Guess what? They do.

That they needed this study, speaks to the researchers not having any awareness about the children who are ripped from their homes – their place of security – and dumped in a strange setting with unfamiliar people caring for them.

Stories abound about abusive foster homes, and many of these kids have heard about them, or even lived in some of them. It would have been more productive to study how to better monitor these homes.

One of the most destructive recent trends in the judicial system is treating juveniles as adults. There is good reason why, in a saner time, we recognized that kids do not have the same capacity for control as adults, and we responded accordingly.

Programs That Work

Tucked away in a rural area is a long-term detention facility for boys that is successfully doing what we often hear cannot be done.

Located in a beautiful mountain setting, the kids enjoy a daily schedule of hiking, kayaking, and tree-rope courses. As we watch schools all around us drop programs that provide healthy ways for our young people to expend energy, this facility for troubled boys gives priority to that release.

But doesn't spending time in physical activity impact negatively on the youngster's grades? Isn't that what we hear from the public schools – that the time must be spent on measurable learning?

The answer can be found in the average score these students obtained on the statewide recent regents exams this past spring. It was 90% – a higher score than many general population schools. Don't all of us perform better when we are not burdened with pent up energy, when we are enjoying an inner calm??

The success of this long-term facility is telling us something about our educational approach generally. If they can receive such positive results with a population of kids who have a history of truanting and "acting out," what can the general population schools achieve if they made meaningful curriculum changes? Perhaps school authorities should begin by asking, if adults need breaks to be productive, how can we ask any less from our more energetic youngsters? They might continue by addressing how creative schools (and home-schooled youth) expand their horizons by fueling the curiosity of those in their care. They might even consider how students retain more information when not pressured to memorize for a test – forgetting most of it a day later. Isn't the goal of education still to nurture curiosity and to have students retain what they are taught? Or has the goal become simply to assure the financial preservation of the school?

Does it make sense to preserve our current approach of curtailing sports, art, and music, in the name of teaching to the test, then medicate kids for presumed ADHD when they are restless in the classroom? Or is it better to incorporate physical activity, community involvement, and passion into the curriculum?

✄

The Sanctuary Model

In 1980 Sandra Bloom (a Psychiatrist) together with Joseph Foderaro (a Social Worker), and Ruth Ann Ryan (a Nurse Manager) designed a program called Sanctuary. Its premise was that to heal, a child needs to be in a safe environment – physically and emotionally.

The Sanctuary Model is a way of changing a facility's culture in order to effectively provide a cohesive setting for healing. Youth meet periodically in the course of the day and provide support for each other. Staff meet daily to maintain a dialogue about the kids they are there to help and explore their own feelings about them. At any time of the day, a child who is feeling stressed may call out "Circle," and other youth surround that child with a circle of support. No questions asked.

Their approach is a total overhaul of the way we usually help (or try to help) troubled youth. It is introspective and responsive. Frequent meetings permit

125

staff to make continuous adjustments to meet the needs of the youth . . . and their own needs. It stands in sharp contrast to where I worked. There we almost never had meetings because the director didn't like meetings.

✾

I remember a very responsive co-worker telling me of a new admission on his way. The staff person had a newborn child, and the admission was court-ordered to detention for child molestation. She said that she thought she would have trouble working with him, being that she had a new baby.

So the two of us – caring people who were able to acknowledge our own vulnerabilities – sat down to discuss how to be there for this boy. We agreed that I would take on most of the interactions, since my child was grown and I would find it less difficult to work with the youth.

This was an informal (and simplified) application of the Sanctuary model. It came about because of the trust and respect between me and the other staff person. There were so many other instances where this did not happen, to the detriment of the youngsters entrusted to our care. It should have happened all the time through frequent meetings, which is the backbone of the Sanctuary model. Why didn't it?

It is also a way to create an environment that attracts employees who want to help and are comfortable enough in their own self to be able to introspect, adapt, change. Good, caring people are drawn to stimulating work environments.

When a facility encourages staff dialogue, when they provide a stimulating environment, they attract (and

James Hudziak, MD -- The Vermont Center for Children, Youth, and Families

Dr. Hudziak is a geneticist. It is common for genetics to be used as a justification for the administration of psychotropic medication to struggling adolescents. After all, "It's in the genes, so what alternatives are there."

Dr. Hudziak sees it differently – dramatically so.

The field of genetics is relatively young and growing rapidly. While there are new discoveries every day, I don't think anyone could have anticipated Dr. Hudziak's recent findings.

Unlike the Missouri system, this is complicated. But, in a nutshell, while it has been documented that genetics can influence environment, Dr. Hudziak has now demonstrated that environment causes measurable *physical* changes in the genetic make-up of an individual. The genes of a child growing up in a highly dysfunctional home, for example, will actually change in configuration. Tension in the home, screaming, abusive behavior – that environment actually changes the physical genotype of the child.

Pragmatically, this means that if you treat the child in their home setting without treating the family, the child will suffer deterioration not only in behavior, but in genetic structure as well. Provide a calm and nurturing setting, and they will respond with healthy development -- mentally, physically, and genetically.

There's more. The thickness of the pre-frontal cortex of the brain of an adolescent is physically affected by the amount of time spent in front of screens – video games, television, cell phones, and others. The more time, the more negative the change! (The average

American teen spends 7.6 hours a day in front of a screen.) Shocking! And now with documentation of the damage.

The good news, of course, is that a child with a healthy, creative, physically active lifestyle will derive the benefit of positive physical changes. There is an international movement called, "No Child Left Inside," an obvious take-off on the destructive school program called, "No Child Left Behind." Started by Richard Louve, it is an attempt to promote the infusion of nature-based programs into curricula everywhere.

It is as simple as encouraging art, music, sports and nature participation into a child's life. And that, of course, presupposes less time in front of screens.

At Dr. Hudziak's Vermont Center for Children, Youth, and Families, a prerequisite for care is that the entire family be involved. A true family-based approach.

Focus is on preserving wellness whenever possible. Reading, sports, art and music are all incorporated into the plan, which is designed by a Family Wellness Coach who visits the family at home and teaches techniques for promoting sound practices.

Psychotropic drugs are utilized in rare instances, and even then kept to a minimum.

It may be redundant, but family time, regardless of schedule, is critical to wellness. Families must find the time to read together, sing together, play sports together. This creates an environment of peace, and gives a growing child the security and release of energy that is desperately needed for success in life.

✄

The Hawn Foundation

The Hawn Foundation recognizes the connection between the self-esteem of our youth and their performance in school. The organization, started by actress Goldie Hawn, offers programs that help children lead ". . . confident, happy, and successful lives." It began in 2003 in response to the rising rate of teen depression, stress, and suicide.

Some years ago educators identified the deleterious effect of an empty stomach on the ability of a child to learn in school. Now it appears that we are finally beginning to realize that a stressed child does not learn as well as a calm, self-assured child. There is a strong correlation between grades, and the implementation of this program called MindUp. The beauty is in its simplicity, and that it has proven success. It awakens the child's senses, reduces stress, and creates a thirst for knowledge. It offers assistance to schools that want it and, given its measurable success, and the small amount of time it takes for daily implementation, it should be a part of every school curriculum.

Read about it in Goldie's book, "10 Mindful Minutes: Giving Our Children--and Ourselves--the Social and Emotional Skills to Reduce Stress and Anxiety for Healthier, Happier Lives," then read about the work of the foundation at: http://thehawnfoundation.org. Finally (perhaps after reviewing the advocacy section of this book), arrange to meet with your child's school administration and advocate for this program in their school. As a dear friend of mine, Maggie Kuhn, once said (and is often quoted), "Stand before the people you fear and speak your mind -- even if your voice shakes."

Contact me and we will do it together. Our children are worth it!

✂

Building Hope for Struggling Youth

Every youngster, no matter how beaten down by circumstance, has within them a spark of life that can only be extinguished in death. That spark is often so well camouflaged, so hidden from others, that it takes a skilled and caring person to detect it. But once it is revealed and built upon, it opens doors to all things good. The problem behaviors of old gradually fall away because they are no longer of value, they are no longer needed.

While it may be sometimes difficult, there are clues to finding a self-protected child's passion. You may see it in their eyes, or in a casual comment. It may be in a request for a certain type of magazine, a specific book, or an unusual attentiveness to a certain television program. It can even be in their working harder on a particular chore.

Once identified, next comes exposure. For a child interested in cooking, for example, ask for their help in the kitchen. Then arrange a visit to a restaurant kitchen during mealtime. For an artistic child, check local museums for special youth-oriented programs. If the child is not able to be with the general population because of poor social skills, call the museum, explain the circumstances, and ask for a private tour. Most will oblige because they share the same passion. Then visit schools with curricula built around the child's interest.

Gently cultivate that interest, being especially perceptive to the child's rate of acceptance. Remember, these kids are self-protective beyond the norm. Let them absorb the possibility of an improved lifestyle at their own comfortable rate.

�֎

Advocacy: Creating Change

Whether we have children of our own or not, we are impacted by how society treats them, by how they develop. When we help a stressed child to overcome adversity by teaching the skills they need, we are reducing crime and saving a young life. It is also cost effective. Not only will that child not be a financial burden to society as an incarcerated adult, or an individual dependent on public services for survival, they will be a contributor to society through their gainful employment -- the taxes they pay and the purchases they make.

It's not easy to advocate for youth. A significant number of adults prefer talking about the spoiled, lazy and rotten kids of today. "Where are the kids of the good old days?" is an often heard refrain. "Kids today have it made!" is another.

Advocacy is something we all have opportunities to do. It can be speaking out about the pressures kids are under, like growing up in single parent homes (or where parents work more than one job), about the schools pushing kids harder than they ever have before, or where psychiatric diagnosis is increasingly erroneous and psychotropics are used irresponsibly. We can help people to understand that all of this is piled on top of the universal adolescent stresses of peer pressure, pleas for acceptance, and the inherent tensions of growing into adulthood.

There is also a desperate need for stressed youth to have someone in their lives who is simply there for

135

them. You can link up with these kids through any of the mentoring programs in your area. But do it only if you are in for the long haul . . . continuity of caring, remember?

Adult stereotypes of stressed youth are hard to break, but that's really an important step toward helping them. (One girl once said to me, "You adults . . . it's like you're stuck.") Because the news media often presents troubled youth in villainous ways, that is a good place to start.

When you read an article, or hear a news item that defames youth using a broad brush, challenge it. Write a letter to the editor, e-mail the publisher, use whatever means possible to show your opposition. Some of my letters to the editor appear later.

Challenge the school, if circumstances warrant. Fight for your school to keep (or reinstate) healthy expressive programs. If you are told there is no money, go to your congressional representative and ask (demand?) funding. They need your vote. Any library will tell you who they are and how to contact them. Be specific, and go (or write) with other constituents if possible. There is strength in numbers.

Petitions to preserve (or reinstate) valuable programs are also effective. But take them to the news media before you turn them in to the school, where they might otherwise be buried. Publicity should be used to your advantage. Media is attracted to concise arguments, where possible documented with facts (and their sources). They also love photo ops.

Approach local radio and television shows about well-targeted, very specific issues and ask for air time. Be sure to check the history – the track record – of the media because some will surprise you with an opposing guest. Also reach out to community publications, asking for articles to be written. Gather facts before you approach them and, if possible, find others who have been in your situation. They like statistics, and also a human angle from someone who has been victimized.

⌘

If you have children in school, get copies of their records! You have a right to them, and a parental responsibility to know what has been said about your child, because it will follow them and surface at the most unexpected times.

⌘

Consider starting a self-help group for parents. Even better, help your kids (and those of others) to start one for themselves. Guide them, but do not control it. Empower them at every step of their development!

⌘

Be there for your friends, family, and neighbors who need emotional support to advocate for their youngsters – to buck the system.

E-mail me, and I will guide you through the formulation of a meaningful approach. I will help in every way possible, because our kids are that important and if we "stand united, we cannot be divided."

⌘

One message we get from the many instances of authoritarian abuse cited in this book, is that parents need support and encouragement if they are to advocate for their children. It can come from a friend, relative or other individual. It can come from you!

The paternal need to protect our children is so strong, that it often undermines our ability to think rationally. All it takes is an authority figure – be it a doctor, teacher, or principal – and we fall into compliance, for fear that to do otherwise would be to place our child in jeopardy. You can be that reality base to those parents.

✄

Hearing from the Reader

I am eager to hear from you, whether you are a parent, teacher, youth worker, or simply a concerned individual who cares about our youth. I want to hear about good and bad experiences, successful and unsuccessful use of medication, fights you have fought . . . and whether you won or lost.

I will also welcome any opportunity to speak to concerned audiences, large or small, that may help to make this world more welcoming to our young people, preferably in a participatory workshop setting.

Mostly, I encourage parents to contact me if they feel they are losing their child. The sooner the better! We are in this struggle together to build a better world . . . a more welcoming and understanding world for our youth, whether they are yours, your neighbor's, or a child you read about somewhere . . . anywhere. You can reach me at irvwestyouthadvocate@yahoo.com

✄

A Sampling of Letters to Solso about Hope and His Future

Dear Solso, (appears on Page 36)

I thought about you yesterday. Actually, I think about you every time I am at the goat farm and they ask about you and remind me that they would hire you in a second to work with the animals. But more about the farm later.

Yesterday, my wife and I did a hike (at our age, we call it a hike to keep our spirits up – but it's more of a walk). We went on a trail that was about a half mile long, along the side of a mountain. Then, almost magically, the trail opened up to a beautiful pond, without a house or other structure to be seen (or heard). It was so peaceful and, as we were just relaxing, we spotted a muskrat lodge (do you know how to tell the difference between a beaver lodge and a muskrat's?), and two ducks swimming in formation on the other end of the pond (we needed our binoculars to spot them).

So why did I think of you? Well, other than the sensitivity that I know you have, I remember you saying how you felt calmness in this area. Most of us feel that. Nature and animals give us that. And I was feeling it big time at that pond.

We walked along the shore, spotted many varieties of mushrooms, tall grass growing in the water – so tall that it flopped over and the top foot or so floated (the grass did not have the strong stems to hold it upright like land-based plants have. Everything in nature really is connected, because the floating part of the grass made a great protective habitat for fish and frogs and

139

stuff. We all (people included) need protection at times. Sometimes from ourselves, other times from predators.

It was a great location, and if you and I ever connect again locally, I would like to show it to you.

Now back to the goat farm, with an update. The male llama jumped the fence, ran a mile down the road to the cemetery, and ate all the flowers families had put on the graves. It took them hours to catch him. Then when he was back home, he harassed the goats in his paddock. So their first thought was to sell the llamas, but I talked them into having the males gelded (neutered). They agreed, but since I have not spoken to them recently, I do not know whether it helped. Sorry, Solso, but for now this is a story without an ending.

My animals are fine; Critter Llama continues to believe he is the best thing that was ever created, and next week he will return (by invitation) to the fiddler's Jamboree, where he will kiss everyone (even those who don't want to be kissed by a 350 pound animal). But I have to make sure I get him out of there before the music starts. I remember last year I didn't get out in time, and the music made him really bug. He is more of a "jazz llama," than a fiddle one.

I hope you are well, and things are coming together. You have very real strengths, including a sharp sense of humor, and deep sensitivity. Both strong qualities. You deserve a strong and rewarding life, and I very much want it for you.

I will stop now because I really do not even know if this letter will find you and, if it does, whether you want this type of communication. If the answer to both is "yes," then write back to me, and I would love to set up a regular correspondence. That would not only make me happy, but also allow me to give the goat farm people some real answers when they inquire about you.

Hey, they welcome all of us, but you are the only one they specifically ask about. You Solso. They only ask about you. Why do you think that is?

With good thoughts and good Wishes,

Irv West

✄

Dear Solso,

I was very happy to get your letter, and especially to hear that you are doing well.

Now I can give you an update from the goat farm, because I took some kids to visit there a couple of weeks ago. Their llamas have calmed down and are now in the large area with the goats. That is the good news. The bad news is that they are not doing their job of keeping the coyotes away. The reason Lorraine and Sheila bought them, is because they lose many goats to predation. Llamas are great at protecting herds, but they should have been sold gelded llamas, and were not. Gelding them later does not work.

So they will keep the llamas because they are caring people (remember how they have a special area for no longer productive goats to live out their lives?), and get a couple of guard dogs for protection.

When you do get back to this area, we can certainly talk with Sheila and Lorraine about your working there, but I also see other possibilities for you. I would especially like to see you working with youth in distress, helping them to get their lives together. I think you would be great at that, be able to apply your life experience, and relate to them in a very meaningful way. There is lots of time to talk of possibilities... as long as you keep those possibilities in your heart and mind starting today and going forward. Having a strong vision for your future is very important! And it should be kept in your heart and mind. Not one place, but both. In other words, feel it and think about it.

Freida and I did another trail Sunday and, again, I thought of you. This one was in the middle of a very populated area. The trail head was right in the middle of a huge and expensive housing development (we were turned off by that at first). But a few feet into the woods, you see the Hudson River way down a ledge, and you continue along a winding path. Then you go over a footbridge (tons of damsel flies there) and the trail goes between two giant hills, one on each side of you. It is closed in and protected from harsh weather so, where all the ferns we had passed had turned brown, in this crevice they were still green. Every hike exposes new mysteries and fascinations of nature.

I gave your good wishes to the staff at detention, and to Critter. The staff was happy to hear you are doing so well, but Critter kind of looked at me with that look that says, "Why do you talk so much... why don't you just feed me?" He liked Fiddler's Jamboree, and this time I was careful to get him out before the music started. One little girl so much wanted to pet him, but every time she tried he would turn to kiss her and she got scared. Oh yea, when I was talking to someone who I knew, someone else said, "Irv look at your llama." He was eating all the lettuce they had laid out for their burger barbecue. So, Solso, do you think he will still get invited back next year?

We are finally getting some solid rainy days here. I was getting worried about the drought. Where I live we get our water from a well, and there is always the possibility of it going dry. Did I ever show you the short *tape about the Heifer Project, the organization I volunteer with? It shows young children carrying water in large cans for miles, because they do not have running water in their homes. I think of that often, and try not to waste food or water. I eat leftovers, and don't leave the water faucet running any more than necessary. I believe that if each of us would feel more of a connection to people around us, we would all benefit. I also try to save fuel by combining trips, but that is not only for conservation reasons but also because of the expense of gas.*

What type of school system do you have there? How often do you go, and do you think it is good? Any science or nature classes? What about art and music? And what about the food? Would a vegetarian like me survive there?

So you turned 16. Wow! Putting your life together at that age means there are many years ahead of you to enjoy, and to do things that make you feel worthwhile and valuable. You are worthwhile and you are valuable, and you have surely earned the right to a very good life. I will help you get that life. I promise. Critter might help to, but I can't promise that.

Finally, I will tell you that Casanova Llama was very sick, but is fine now. He is old, but has always been in good health. One day he stopped eating, a sign that something is wrong. Llamas will not even skip one meal. The vet came out, gave him an appetite stimulant, a shot of vitamin B12 (I take that because the vitamin is found in meat and vegetarians are deficient in it), and something else that I don't remember. The next day he woke up ready to catch up on the meals he had missed. He is back to bossing the others around which, for him, is a sign of his good health.

That's all for now. I will watch my mailbox for a letter from you, and feel good when it arrives.

Hayua (which means peace), Irv West

✄

Dear Solso,

I have not yet received your letter, but did get the message about how well things are going.

Saturday, I did a workshop for Caritas (we send volunteers to very sick people's homes to give support and help). My part was to teach them how to really listen. It is called Active Listening. And I thought of you because I always tried to really, really, really listen to you: To your joys, your hopes, and, yes, to your pain.

It is always good to hear from you, but it was exciting to hear how well you are doing. Still, I want to be there for you through the good and the bad – we all have a range of emotions.

Yesterday I took Critter Llama out to greet some of the people going to the maple syrup open houses. There is one just down the road here. He caused a traffic jam, with everyone stopping to meet him. Of course Critter reached in every car and kissed all the occupants (front seat and back)!

Then a man stopped who was a little uncomfortable with such a large animal at his car (even though he had stopped and did not have to), so he kept his window closed. Critter was in a kissing frenzy by that time, so he went to kiss the guy and hit his snout on the window. Neither the window nor the Crit was hurt, and the guy thought it was so funny that he rolled it down and got kissed.

It will take time for you to smooth out the rough edges and build on your strengths. You have so many strengths, Solso, from a real sensitivity to others, to the intelligence to know how to apply it. You have also given me insights, which I have used to reach other youth. That's powerful.

So keep in touch with me, and let me know how the visit to the llama farm goes. Especially as compared to Morgan's farm. I suspect it will be smaller, but they may be doing some things differently and it will be interesting to compare. And, yes, your picture is STILL hanging on the barn wall.

Tomorrow, I am taking a computer class at the library. It is free, and they teach you whatever you ask... whatever you don't know. For me, that is everything from the time I turn on the machine, until the time I turn it off. Well, that is an exaggeration, but I am NOT good at technology. Not at all! I still don't even know how to use my horrible cell phone.

Be well, my child, and keep in touch. I promise to write again soon.

HAYUA, Mr. West

�֎

Dear Solso,

Thanks for your letter, Solso.

So much is happening in your life. Not many people (let alone young people) have their art displayed in a well-known museum. And that IS a well-known place. You are also in a steel band?

It must be so painful to see a further separation with your dad. I can't really fully relate to it, but I can in one way. My father put me down all the time and, what finally saved me was when I left and was raised by two very loving people who acted as my foster parents. I never really wanted any connection with my parents after that, but I know that you do. I personally do not think it is meant to be. I know he loves you... I'm sure he does... but I am just as sure that he has his own overwhelming problems that do not let him express his love. There are many people who care deeply about you, Solso, including me. They see a great future for you, and minor set-backs (that we all have) do not change that one bit. Hang with the ones who care.

I took Critter out on the road last Sunday. It was maple syrup open house so there were lots of tourists. Most of them stopped and opened their window. Critter kissed every single person he could reach. Then, this guy stopped who was not too comfortable around him, so he kept his window closed. Critter didn't realize this, so he reached in to kiss him and whacked his snout against the glass. The guy laughed, and Crit was so embarrassed that he tried to go back home by himself.

I do not want to bring Critter Llama to the youth fair because I don't want him in the hot sun for hours. We are also going to make it easier to find events and exhibits, with big signs. To me it seems to get better every year. We used to make it a regular agricultural

146

fair, like other nearby counties have. But they have many, many farms, and we do not. So no one wanted to come to our fair. Ever since we made it a youth fair, attendance has been going up. But so has Georgia's stress level, because she does most of the work. Other staff pick on her. Sometimes people pick on others because they are really insecure and, by finding faults in others, it makes them feel superior. Very twisted logic, huh?

Hey, that reminds me: the library now has weekly meetings for youth. They call it "Twisted Teens." They write poetry, read, watch films, etc. It sounds good, and the guy who runs it really likes young people.

Stay well, Solso, and keep building. And, when you have a dip, give it perspective. We all have them. All of us!

I will try to write at least once a week, and also continue to work on getting on your call list.

Hayua, Mr. West

✂

Dear Solso,

I told you that I would write about once a week.

Most of the snow here is gone, and little green thingys are popping up in the garden. Unfortunately my roto-tiller, which grinds up the soil before planting, died and went to heaven (or somewhere, I am not sure). It was old, but not as old as me. So I have to decide whether to give up the garden, buy a cheap low power one, or rent a good one for a day. I can't afford to buy a powerful one like the old one was.

The llamas are now enjoying that they can cush (lay

down) on the ground, and not get their big bellies covered with snow. Not that they really mind it. They don't mind much... they kind of take everything in stride.

Georgia has moved to her new room at work, and it has made her grumpy. More grumpy than usual. She will recover and continue to do the fantastic job she always has done with public relations. She asks about you all the time.

I know that you have good times and bad, Solso, and both are times to be respected. Oh, how many times I wish I had a magic wand, capable of turning the bad ones to good. But each has to run its course and, as long as you work on encouraging the good, the bad times will show up less and less often. They will never be totally gone, you know, not for any of us. But life is about getting all the good things we need to feel fulfilled, to feel whole. You will get there... I know it.

One of my heroes is a guy named Robert Brooks. He is a famous psychologist who is really down to earth. He says that a person has to build on their "*island of strength*." Actually he called it "island of competence," but I like my version better. What parents do too often is to tear at all the problems, never giving recognition to the good stuff... the strength part. You have to do it, Solso, whether it be with a pencil and paper, or just in your mind. Think of your strengths and how they will carry you through the good and bad times. If I were making a list of your strengths, I would need a full ream of paper (I think a ream is 500 sheets). It is those strengths that will carry you to a wonderful life. Build on them, nurture them, and watch them grow.

I'll start you off: you have an incredible sensitivity to others, and to your own feelings. You take it from there. The list does not have to be long, just strong. It will be strong. I chose the right kid to be adopted by. I know that I did.

Tomorrow I am having lunch with a young lady who now has two young children. She had a very rough time in her early years, Solso... a very rough time. She was in my Trekin' Llama 4-H club and had a special way with the animals. Well, now she is doing great, and she attributes it to me. SHE IS WRONG! SHE did it, just as you will. All I did was to give her the comfort in herself to know she can make it – correct that to read that she WILL make it. And she did.

So we will eat pizza and talk, and eat more and talk more. But you know what is soooo unfair? Well, whether I helped her turn her life around or not, still I have to buy the pizza. Imagine that!

Hey, be careful when you play ball, and don't damage anything. And listen to the birds coming back from their migration, because they are singing to you. If you listen very carefully, you will learn that they, too, like Alicia Keys and are singing: "Everything is gonna be all right."

I will write again next week.

Hayua, Irv West

P.S. I have enclosed a letter I wrote to the Post Star about something they said that pretty much trashed young people's values. I hate when that is done.

✂

BREAKING THE RULES

Dear Solso,

I really hope that this letter reaches you. The only reason you did not hear from me sooner is that the Rochester facility rejected my letters to you, and sent them back to me.

I hope that you are well, and putting together the good life that you so deserve.

So where did we leave off? Well, I am back in school studying adolescent counseling. Pretty crazy for someone my age, huh?

Casanova Llama had cancer and I had to put him down. It is always such a hard thing to do, but is best for the animal. Did I ever tell you that llamas hide their pain? Their instincts tell them to, because if they did not, then a prey animal (like a coyote) would go after them. Showing pain is saying that they are weak and can be more easily caught. I do know he was suffering, and is now at peace.

After he was down, Lima and Critter did a llama funeral which is quite common. They surround the body and hum... which is a sign of distress for a llama. Then, for the next few days, Critter tried to become the boss llama. But Lima would not permit it, and there was some heavy spitting between them. I think it would be cool if people could stop bombing people and just spit instead.

Critter is getting restless, so I think I will get him a couple of goats to herd. They will come from the goat farm we visited, the place that offered you a job.

I also got 2 new cats and they get along great. One had been bullied by the others.

Enough about me. How are you and where are you? And what have you been doing? I think of you often, Solso, and remember both the good conversations and the outings that we shared.

Solso, I wish you Neebi (A Kenyan word of wishes for a life free of danger, menace, uncertainty and fear), I would also love to hear from you.

Irv West

�֎

Samples of Letters to the Editor Advocating for our Youth

EDITOR:

An adolescent girl recently left me a voice mail. She said I probably did not remember her, that she was in detention more than 2 years ago, where I worked as a counselor. She explained that she graduated from high school yesterday, and will tell me more when I call her, which I certainly will do.

I plan to tell her how, having accomplished so much already, she can now take on almost anything and be successful; I will tell her I certainly do remember her, which I do; I also remember telling her then that I believed very much in her, but I did not think that she believed in herself. I will tell her that now I think she does.

How dare you write your recent editorial demeaning the accomplishment of our young people's graduations with statements like: "a high school diploma is hardly worth the paper it's printed on . . . ," and "what is coming is more difficult, more complex, and more difficult to reverse." Your diatribe is enough to scare any young person.

Why do we need to lecture our young people so much? Why do we find it so hard to give them support and encouragement instead? A recent article in *Join Together* (a daily summary of national articles about youth), cited a study that found young people who are given structure and warmth (substitute support), avoid using drugs in far greater numbers than those in an authoritarian setting.

This girl wanted to share her good feelings with someone she had not been in contact with for more than two years, but who had expressed caring for her. She remembered! I am not going to denigrate her accomplishment, but instead will build on it. You owe her, and every other recent graduate, an apology!

IRV WEST

✂

EDITOR:

I work at a short-term residential home for youth. Because idle time really does weigh heavily on this population, I like to get them out at every opportunity. So, on a beautiful summer day, we grabbed tennis rackets and headed for a town with a few asphalt-surfaced tennis courts.

Leaving the van, we noticed some kids biking and skateboarding on the courts. They had ramps, were laughing and sharing . . . having a good time. When they saw us approaching, rackets in hand, they said they would clear off one of the courts for us. We thanked them. We were having fun and they were having fun. In fact, one of the skateboarders retrieved our stray balls . . . and there were many.

After a while, we moved on to something else. The kids politely accepted our thanks for their responsiveness, and returned to their activity.

As we were leaving, a man appeared with his young daughter, like us, with tennis rackets in hand. He immediately launched a tirade against these youth for using the area for other than what it was intended.

Without responding, the kids packed up their equipment and, ramps in tow, they left.

It is worth noting that this town offers nothing else in the way of recreation. No swimming pool, no designated skateboarding parks . . . nothing else.

If any of those kids read this letter, I would like to thank them for demonstrating maturity, and acting in a courteous and considerate manner. If the man who yelled at them reads this, I would like to suggest he rethink his approach to youth who demonstrate all of these most admirable of character traits. He might also think about the message his behavior conveyed to his daughter.

IRV WEST

�֎

EDITOR:

On May 19, 2011, there was a deeply moving tree planting ceremony in memory of a teen who committed suicide one year earlier. More than 50 people attended, there were tears shed, bonds formed, memories relived. Despite the frightening rise in teen suicides in the area, the Post Star chose not to cover it, so I would like to relay the important messages delivered at that event.

Both Courtney's mom, and a friend of the family, spoke movingly about how the pain of loss lingers in survivors -- how suicide leaves a scar in the lives of friends and family that is slow to heal.

Amy Molloy, representing the Foundation for Suicide Prevention, told us about the availability of help to ease the pain for someone contemplating ending their life.

She emphasized that there are many caring, well-trained people eager to help.

I spoke about the importance of parents listening non-judgmentally to their children, and advocating for them when schools and health practices do not act in their interest. I talked about the misuse of psychotropic medications, the frequent misdiagnosis of psychological ailments, and I stressed the importance of parents routinely getting copies of school and health records because they often hold surprises parents should know about. You have a right to those records.

It is important for our young people to know that many of us do care, and are able to really hear them. If a young person is depressed and not sure where to turn, they should immediately contact someone they trust. That can be a school counselor, pastor, friend or relative. Finding the right person, the right support, will be a step toward assuring that the pain will stop, and life will be all that it should be. Our young people deserve nothing less.

IRV WEST

�֍

EDITOR:

It's not unusual for me to receive a phone call late at night from a youth who is stressed. And while I'm happy to set aside my much needed rest and listen to them – *really hear* what they are saying – I also lament that there's no one in their immediate family they can turn to.

Our children are growing up in the hardest of times. Drugs and alcohol are readily available, schools push them to achieve at a manic pace, and so often they feel estranged from their families. There are just too many single moms raising families (it wasn't meant to be that way), and the financial need to work long hours (often more than one job) leaves parents so exhausted that they are oblivious to their teen's cries for help, and miss critical cues.

Your editorial favoring keeping a gym open in Fort Ann – providing an opportunity for youngsters and their parents to enjoy time together, was right on the mark. It reminded me of the time I was running the parenting program at the YMCA. Before class I would chat with a young girl, the daughter of a single mom who worked there. This girl was obese, and suffered very low self-esteem. One day I invited her to speak to the class so parents would hear a youth's perspective, and she accepted. What she chose to say speaks volumes: "Do you know how we kids feel when we come home from school and say 'Mom, I've got to talk to you,' and you say, 'Okay talk to me while I wash the dishes.'"

Think about it. Of all the things she could have brought up, she chose to speak about feeling secondary to a household chore.

IRV WEST

�֎

EDITOR:

In the November 12, 2011 edition of the Post Star you reported that, of the 4,685 schools in New York State, 1,325 schools were cited as not meeting standards. So where do we go from here?

BREAKING THE RULES

Do we follow the same route of eliminating those activities like music, art and sports – those subjects that act as a release of energy and tension for our youngsters, and continue the same old same old hoping for different results? Or do we look to schools and social programs that have demonstrated great success with their fresh approach? Will we confront our young people with their failures (aren't they really *our* failures?), or build their self-esteem so they know they can succeed? Is there even time in the curriculum for esteem-building, or has that been dropped because it is not a mandated subject?

We are at yet another crossroads, only this time there are healthy, successful models for us to emulate. If we choose the same misinformed road and wonder why the school drop-out rate continues to rise and our youth turn to chemical release, we have committed a horrible atrocity on our kids.

I hope that we opt to study the success of the Kipps program, and ask why a responsive long-term detention facility in our area had a higher Regents average than many of our general population schools. My fear is that it will not happen and, if asked, the educational bureaucracy will offer the lame excuses that they are not comparable.

I plead with every parent to watch the DVD, "Waiting for Superman," Google kipp.org, then get involved in the fight to hold the school system's hierarchy accountable to our kids, before it's too late.

IRV WEST

✄

EDITOR:

Both in my vocation and my avocation I am in contact with young people who are trying to cope with stresses in their lives, including many imposed on them by society. They often tell me that their greatest stress reducer is participating in sports.

Whenever I hear that, it brings me back to my own childhood, where I spent almost every weeknight at the local school in the gym. There was a basketball court, some table games and, oh yes, one staff person who could sense almost instinctively when one of us needed to talk.

Pressures on our youngsters in recent years have increased exponentially. But now, at least in Warrensburg, instead of spending the small amount of money to keep a school open and have it provide evening activities, we have police officers enforcing a curfew, even though the kids have nowhere else to go. No escape from what is often a non-supportive (or even destructive) home environment; no recreation except for a T.V. and video games; no one with that "instinct" to sense when there is a problem, where parents (and others) may have missed it.

It seems like strange priorities to me.

IRV WEST

�֎

EDITOR:

In a recent "Ask Mr. Dad" column, the author responded to a query saying, "It's absolutely impossible to spoil a baby that young" (the child in question was two-months old). I would suggest that it is impossible to "spoil" (or, more commonly stated "spoil rotten") a child of any age.

In my parenting counseling, I discourage parents from using words like "spoiled" or "rotten" in our discussions. These are two irreversible processes. Children have problems, stresses, behavioral issues, all of which are, indeed, reversible.

There is great meaning conveyed by the words we choose.

Here's another example. Why is a child in DSS' (Department of Social Services) custody assigned a "case" worker. Is that child truly a "case"? A better option would be a "care" worker. In my work with at-risk youth, I cringe every time one of my kids asks to call their "case" worker, I guess because I see each as an individual -- not a case. And I care.

IRV WEST

❁

EDITOR:

Are we adults contributing to the rash of teenage suicides? Are we strong enough in ourselves to introspect, and determine if there is something we should do differently?

Our current approach to educational reform is premised on any child who does not conform to a norm (often at the expense of having to deny their individual rates of growth and development), being labeled, diagnosed and, too-often, medicated. By so doing, we unintentionally give license to youth who pick on the non-conforming child, whether because of sexual orientation, foreign accent, or their need for special help. In all these instances, the bullier isolates the one aspect that sets the child aside (their individuality), and moves in for (sometimes literally) the kill.

There were four recent suicides in one Ohio school, each victim seeking release from pain. A number of students at that school specifically attributed the deaths to "a culture of conformity." Are these kids more perceptive than we? Often they are, but we don't listen!

Let's rethink our educational approach, discard "Race To The Top" (education shouldn't be a race), encourage kids to develop at their own rate, drastically reduce reliance on psychotropic drugs (recognizing it as an often misguided tool to simply pacify our youth). While we're at it, let's teach to each child's strengths, not some amorphous norm. Finally, instead of resorting to our default mechanism of punishing the bullier, let's impose consequences fitting their actions, and provide help to overcome their need to subjugate a peer. Costly? So is suicide!

If we're serious about change, then we have an incredible template in how Missouri has addressed bullying (as well as all other aspects of helping wounded youth). I write a great deal about that in my soon to be published book.

Let's save young lives!

IRV WEST

✄

Letters: **Psychotropic drugging is easy, but it's abuse, not a cure**

To the editor:

Thank you so very much for the article on the use (misuse?) of psychotropic medications for young people.

I work with troubled youth, and have seen so many of them drugged into lethargy. Worse, it is considered a "cure," so therapy and other forms of help are withdrawn. The intent is for them to remain a legal addict for life.

There are so many cases I could cite, but I will only give one: a 16-year old girl who was institutionalized for aggression. She had been in a gang and was a school truant. She had been abandoned by her parents in the first week of her life.

During my time with her, I witnessed her passion to cook, and I encouraged it. I arranged for her to visit the kitchen of a well-respected restaurant, brought in recipe books, and because of her culinary skill, we all shared some wonderful meals at the detention facility where she had been placed.

When I presented the possibility of her going to culinary school (AmeriCorps has a wonderful program), she got excited. Her life was, for the first time, coming together because she was now building on what I think of as her "*island of strength*." Every child has one.

When a youngster does not envision a realistic future - a worthy goal to strive toward - they act out, drug out, truant, etc. Why not? They are living in the moment, because they do not believe there is a tomorrow.

It's pretty much what we adults would do if we were told we had only months to live. (I haven't smoked a cigarette in 40 years, but I would buy a pack at the first store I passed.)

During her extended stay at the facility, this girl did not exhibit any aggression. In fact her behavior was positive, enthusiastic, responsive.

Here's the story's sad ending. She went for a routine physical, during which her doctor put her on lithium. She quickly gained weight, became lethargic, and asked me to withdraw her application to culinary school.

It is quite conceivable that this girl will return to her former lifestyle or one similar. What was done to her is immoral, and there are hundreds of other similar stories documenting of this kind of abuse. It is disgraceful that drugs are prescribed because of the influence of pharmaceutical lobbying, and because it is the most expedient way to "deal" with a troubled child.

And for those who do not relate to the morality aspect of this story, think of the fiscal cost of keeping so many of these youngsters in various institutions, often for life. It is obscene on all levels.

Irv West

Letters to Youth

Dear Fiona, (does not appear in the book)

Your letter, in between the problems, which I will get to, was very exciting. Both for reasons you state, and others I found between the lines. I will talk to you about all of it.

First, Fiona, I want to tell you that I am truly honored that you want to keep a line of conversation going with me. I feel very privileged because it means (I think) that you know how much I care about you and how much I see a wonderful future for you.

Let me talk first about your future (you will see that I am using "words" like "talk" instead of "write" because we can't actually speak to each other, so these letters are a substitute).

So you are a peer leader now! Believe it or not, we were doing a group last week -- a video on stress -- and how to respond to it. They made reference to peer leaders, and I immediately thought of you. Then I thought of how well you would do at Amorak Youth Home, helping kids who can't make it without help. You would love it, Fiona, and just as I do, you would leave with a good feeling inside at the end of every shift. So I am offering you that job again, and all you need to do is keep it all straight, and get at least a high school education.

Jackie talks about you a lot. She asks how you are doing, and I pick out the good things and tell her. I consider things like being a peer leader a good thing, but things about your relationship with your mother (I am getting to that) are private and between us. Are you comfortable with that? Or would you prefer that I give a kind of neutral answer like, "she is fine." It is your call.

It must hurt very much to feel that you are less important to your mother than you should be. I would imagine that you were putting a lot of hope into that family session, and then... well... it collapsed. In my childhood I grew up in a cold and uncaring home. Neither of my parents ever said a positive word to me, and later I went in to foster care with wonderfully supportive "parents." They saved my life, and I NEVER looked back.

So where are you right now? You have an offer of a good... a great... job for your future, you are doing well at Columbia, and your home life sucks. As much as I do not like giving advice, let me be your foster dad for a moment (a role that I am comfortable with) and say, let your past go and be especially careful not to let it injure your future. And there's more. If you suffer from some set-backs along the way, work them through, but don't let them get out of proportion. For example, you want to live with your friend. That may not happen... for now. But it can happen sometime in the future. The immediate concern, when the time is right, is where to live where your incredible talents and sensitivity can grow, and be put to use helping others.

We have not heard from Jackie. I had a feeling that would happen, but was hoping I would be wrong. I like being wrong about that type of prediction. I can only hope that she is at Job Corps and doing well.

Sometimes all it takes to turn a life around is someone to believe in you, and for you to have a clear goal. One of my heroes, a down-to-earth psychologist (Robert Brooks), also said you need to focus on your strengths, which parents are usually horrible at doing. They, instead, pick at the problems. He called it your "*island of competence.*" I certainly fill the category of someone who believes in you, so you tell me what's your *island of competence*, Fiona?

BREAKING THE RULES

As to my birthday, thank you for not only remembering, but also getting the age right. As usual, I will light a candle in memory of my pet dinosaur, Sue, and be grateful that, at my age, I can even get out of bed without help.

I will be having lunch tomorrow with a young lady who is now married and has two children. She had a very rough time early on, but put it all together. She says I did it, but she is wrong. So wrong! She did it... I just gave her the comfort to be able to do it. You will too. I know it. Oh, and one more thing. Whether I did it, or she did, I still have to buy the pizza. Now, is that fair?

Keep in touch. I get excited when I see a letter from you. Some day we might even talk to each other again. But try to put the letter in the envelope right side up. I had to stand on my head to read it this time, and that is really difficult for someone my age.

HAYUA, Irv West

P.S. I am enclosing a copy of a letter to the editor I wrote recently. I hate when they put kids down in an article.

❁

Dear Fiona,

I need to begin this letter with an apology of sorts. When I go to Co-op and pick up my mail, often a week might have passed since I was last there. And when there is a letter from you, I always try to answer it at once, because the letter might have been sitting, all alone and lonely, in the box. Well, this time I fell behind, and so this apology.

You also need to know that when there is a letter from you, I sit down, and pick at the flap a bit. I kind of delay opening it, kind of savor the moment, then plunge in. Unlike most of the other mail I get, your letters cannot wait to be read until I am home. That would be too painful. There is a certain magic to getting a letter from someone you care about that is not the same as with an e-mail. You can hold the letter, pick at it, and then read it. You can't do that with a computer screen. Well, you can, but people will think you are crazy.

It must have been a painful decision to give up your boyfriend. You have written to me a good deal about that difficult choice, and talked to me about it often when we shared time at detention. I would imagine that the decision was all the harder because you are away from him right now. But I think that very distance allowed you to think it through more clearly and, I would suspect, make the right choice.

Fiona you _will_ find someone who values you for who you are, and will want to be with you always. Cheating on you will be something beyond their imaginings, because they will recognize how fortunate they are for having found you. I know that these words may sound hollow to you right now, and I can't change that. But I know it will happen.

There are two deep concerns I have in your last letter, and I will speak about the harder one first.

Your relationship with your mom is, clearly, causing you much grief. I can relate to it because, as I have already written to you, I never had a loving relationship with either of my parents, and it nearly destroyed me. Then some people who really cared about me, undid the damage caused by my parents. They eventually became my foster parents.

I do not know much about your relationship with your mom, and I am not able to even guess why she does what she does. But I do know you quite well (I think that you know me the same), and I see an incredible future for you. Let me repeat that: *I see an incredible future for you!!* You need to nurture that thought, to roll it around in your heart and mind, and do whatever it takes to make it a reality. That may – probably does – mean giving up on trying to win your mom over, and letting it go wherever it goes. She may come around later, perhaps she is acting out of guilt, and when you have things going so well, she may feel less guilty. I don't know. Or perhaps she wants to protect you and, possibly, she chooses the wrong ways. It doesn't matter... what matters is you and your future.

Please understand that I am not saying you should break connections with your mom... not at all. I am saying that you need to give it a place, keep it in its place, and that place must not be one that will allow it to take over your whole life, your every waking thought. There are people who care about you, Fiona, and I am among them.

Now here's the easier one. You may not feel that you know your strengths right now but, be assured, that I do, and I will happily keep reminding you of them. They include your strong awareness of what is going on in your life, your wanting to keep helpful communication going (including these letters), your intelligence and clarity of thought, even how you smile first thing when you wake up to face a new day. Your sense of humor also gives perspective to our conversations and, I am sure, those you hold with others. That you are overwhelmed right now with having broken up with your boyfriend, and also about the issues with your mom, does not take anything from your strengths. In fact, it is those very strengths that need to be called on to help you get through the rough times.

I did hear, finally, from Jackie and she is holding

167

things together. I am not able to go further into what is happening, just as I treat your writings as a deep trust, and keep them in confidence between us. I did tell her that you asked about her, and that made her feel good.

Let me close with more details about a story that I already shared with you, but without the details. There was a girl, many years ago, who was in my 4-H group. She had a magical way with the llamas for which I admit to being jealous. Her home life was hell. She never looked me in the eye -- had a really bad self-image. Then she moved in with a guy who drank excessively and got violent when he was drunk. It seemed so gloomy (not a very cool word is it?), and I feared for her future. When she had a baby, the guy married her and decided that he wanted to be a good role model for his son. So he totally gave up drinking and got two jobs so the girl could stay home with their child (they now have two boys). I have become close to the entire family, and they are doing so well. I no longer worry about her future. She looks me right in the eye when she speaks to me.

Write back soon, and stop using those stupid initials for words. I could just as easily write to you: wkvcfsjdsgeik, and that would have summarized this entire letter. Would you like that?

Fiona, I care about you, and want you to have the same life that the girl I wrote about now has.

Hayua, Irv West

P.S. Tell me more about the letters between you and your dad. And draw me a picture . . . of something, anything . . . and send it to me.

Dear Fiona,

I got your letter last night and sat down with my usual eagerness to read it and find out how things are going. I was so eager, in fact, that they had to remind me I was missing the meeting that brought me to Co-op in the first place.

All right, now, be honest. Was it really a fox that ate the chickens, or did you pig out on chicken one evening? The evidence is probably in whether you had a sudden large gain in weight. Did you?

I am sorry that you had a fight (argument) with Cathy. You were good friends, weren't you? Did this end the friendship, or was it a one-time thing? Good friends are hard to find and, sometimes (because you trust them) your emotions – good and bad – come out more quickly. What did you fight about? Was it a small thing or a heavy disagreement?

Now, speaking of friends, here comes the boyfriend part of the letter you wrote about. First, you are wrong, Fiona, men do not cheat because they are men. I have not cheated in my 239 years of life, and I know many others who do not. Men cheat only when they are missing a piece of their conscience. Their hormones take over, and they do not think clearly. Also, if it happened once, it is almost certainly going to happen again. You are special, Fiona, and you deserve better. If he is telling you he does not want to lose you and will not mess up again, kinda makes you wonder why he didn't think of that this last time.

I sure do hope that the home visit goes well. But if it does not, well, you are still going to have all the good things life has to give.

I will ask Jackie if she is comfortable with my telling you what is going on. If she says yes, as I believe she will, then watch for details in my next letter. I can tell you that it is all good news. It will be for you too, in your life.

So you accuse me of being silly sometimes, huh. Is that a good thing or a bad thing? Wasn't I silly at detention on occasion? You didn't seem to mind it then. In fact, I remember some good laughs from you.

Casanova Llama looks really strange with only one normal eye. The other is bright pink and he cannot see from it. It does not seem to bother him at all.

The little llama at the goat farm is doing very poorly. I suggested that they put him down. He is in a tiny space that is making him crazier. It is so sad. But the chickens at the farm are fine, probably because you can't get to them and eat them all. Oops, you haven't been found guilty (yet), have you?

Keep writing. Tell me about the good times and the bad. It is really important to surround yourself with people who care about you. I am definitely one of those people.

And, most important, don't take on other people's problems, whether they are family, boyfriends, or other youth. I know it is easier to say than to do, but keep your future in focus and it will happen.

Please be aware that I care enough about you to be responding to your letter, even though I promised I would not if you use those dumb short cuts to writing. Like in your last letter when you said WB soon. I can only guess that the "WB" stands for "West Breaks" soon. So are you saying that I will be broken soon? At 239 years, you may be right but, still, can't you spell it out?

Irv West

BREAKING THE RULES

Dear Elinor, (appears on Page 52)

Welcome home! You have struggled so hard to get there, and now you have people who care deeply about you.

I want to thank you for your trust. You made me feel special with your choosing me to confide in about your joys, your sorrows, and your fears. You were also an incredible cooking partner. Please do not waver from the goal of being a professional cook. Not everyone is as successful in identifying their *island of strength* -- the passion that they have and the skill to go along with it.

If there was one thing I would like you to keep with you, from the many talks we had and the tears we shed (yes, Elinor, I too, have shed tears for you), it is that there are bound to be disagreements in life because, as I told you, life is not "...a rose garden." And you have not really had practice working through those problems. So if you get angry with Judy, call and bitch to me; if you get angry with me, talk to Judy and bitch about me. But that is after you talk directly to that person and tell them how you are feeling.

And, please. Be patient. The awkward feelings you identified to me about finally having a home and a family will pass in its own time. Don't run from them! Don't run from anything!!

When you are settled in, I will arrange a visit to the restaurant, and will teach you to drive. Both, of course, with the approval of your new mom. And when you are ready, I will open doors for you to get your culinary training.

I know that there are some kids from detention who will want to write to you. Is that all right with you?

Elinor, to have endured all that you have is nothing less than a sign of your strength. To have accomplished that and still have the ability to speak of (and expose) your vulnerabilities, is nothing less than incredible. You are nothing less than incredible. Now let's move forward -- all of us together -- toward building the wonderful life that is waiting for you.   Irv West

�֎

Dear Kara, (appears on Page 16)

You were wondering if I remember you? Of course I do. You are in my soul, child, and that is forever. I even remember you "taking me out" for talking race at the kitchen table. And I still remember your exit interview where you talked about the respect I showed to you and others, when enforcing rules. The truth is that with the respect I had for all the youth, and that I received from them, the rules did not need to be enforced very often. I think that it was easier for me than other staff there, because we talked, disagreed (one of your many strengths), advocated (another of your strengths), and eventually we agreed on everything (well almost everything).

I am excited about *all* the good things you wrote to me about, Kara. Very excited! I knew from the first days that you had such incredible future ahead of you, but I was not sure you recognized it. Now I think you do.

I am no longer at detention. They felt I was being too responsive to the kids, and I felt that there was no such thing as "too responsive." I don't even understand what "too responsive" means, and you will understand what I mean as you read further. Actually, leaving non-secure was a relief, although I miss the kids a great deal, but not the bosses.

Back to you; I hope that you have found healthy outlets for the anger you said you still feel. It needs to have a safe way out, or else it builds up. So let me tell you that I would love for you to call me whenever you want to talk, or for you to write or email. I will put all the contacts at the bottom of this letter. You can pass on good news, stresses, or pick my brains about anything . . . at any time. You can even ask llama questions (DUH!). Call me at 2am or 2pm, and if I do not answer, I will call you back soon. I will also answer any letter you send, regular mail or e-mail, by the next day. Promise. So do you think you are important to me? Am I being "too responsive?"

I am curious how you knew about Casanova's eye. We haven't talked or written in ages, and his eye problem developed recently. Anyway, he had cancer and I had to put him down a few weeks ago. Critter is still having a hard time, because he tried to take over the dominant role, but was too young, and Lima Llama put him in his place (kind of like you did with me a couple of times, although you didn't spit at me). Cassie rests in the backyard and, after he was euthanized, both Lima and Critter lay at the site and hummed (a sign of distress for a llama). Llamas almost always have a "funeral" when a herd member dies. Human adults are pompous – we do not give enough credit to the other animals that share the earth. Just like we also do not really listen and give credit to the wisdom of our young people.

You should be sitting down for some news I have. Well, I am going back to school at the age of 240 (you remember that I was born on April 19, 1769, don't you)? I am going to get certified as a counselor and listen to teens, always with respect, of course, and always with deep caring. Crazy, huh?

Kara, you are special. I have learned more from you and the other youth I have met and talked with, than I have from all the textbooks and classes I have been exposed to. I will always be grateful to you for that.

I am no less grateful for your wanting to share your good news with me. As you continue to grow into the life you will enjoy, please expect some bumps along the way. They are there for all of us. It doesn't mean that you have lost everything you worked so hard for, so please just deal with them one at a time. And, again, I will always be here for you if you wish.

One more way I can help is for me to write a letter of recommendation for you to any colleges you apply to. Let me know. You might also want to consider Empire State College. They are a division of SUNY and you work on setting your own course of study with a mentor. Then you can take courses by email, in small meeting sessions, or even in weekend workshops. They have students all over the world (for example, many soldiers in Iraq are enrolled). The 2 advantages are that you can study in the way that is best for you, and you can take classes when it does not interfere with work or other activities. They are also very cheap and have lots of scholarship money available. One disadvantage is that you must have self-discipline, and for some people the structure of the classroom with regular assignments works better. Only you can know which setting works for you.

I so hope you want to stay in touch. No one else will read what you write, or hear what you say:

So, as we young folks say, CRTFHWTAGFY, or "crying real tears for how well things are going for you."

You said that you always remember people who made you smile, so you remember me. I always remember people who have opened their heart to me, who have taught me about myself, and how to best relate to others. So I will *always* remember you.

Hayua, and Albrazos (hugs in Spanish), Irv West

BREAKING THE RULES

�֍

Dear Kara,

It is Sunday, and I rushed through my chores (like cleaning the barn) so there would be lots of time to do one of the most fun things in the world – answer a "Kara letter."

Here are some more thoughts on the "please" and "thank you" thing. Yea, I know that it is not common to hear kids who are hanging together say those words. It is surely not cool. But there are many important contacts that will come into your life where those words, which you say because they are a habit now, will make a really good impression.

For example, here comes two Kara's for a job interview. It is a really great job (we know you will get a job like that one day), and the man doing the interview asks each Kara to have a seat.

Kara 1, (which is the new you), simply says, "Thank you sir," and sits down.

Kara 2, (which is the before detention one), says "Hey man, coooool," then spins the chair around and sits backwards.

Then the Kara's both develop a bit of a cough (perhaps they are kind of nervous about getting the job). So they say:

Kara 1 (remember, that's you now), "Excuse me, may I please have a glass of water?"

Kara 2 (the old you) says, "Hey man, would you squirt some of that liquid into a round thing and pass it this way?"

So who is most likely to get the job? Yea, it is the new Kara.

Now, we have gotten to know the old Kara quite well, and see a great future for her. So when we say the "new" Kara, it is only about the change to polite manners.

You wrote about being something in life. Well, Kara, you already are a very important part of life and of the people around you. You had a deep effect on the people at detention, and we are sure you do on many others too. And your future is sure to make you proud of all you accomplished, and feel good about each day. Your life is sure to touch many, many others -- we know because you already have here at detention. It is nice, indeed, to know that we have taught you useful skills, but don't ever forget that we have also been privileged to have spent time with you as well.

You also wrote in your last letter about what is usually called a legacy – it is what you leave behind when you die. One type of legacy, the one that to some is most important, is how many people have been helped because you were on this earth. They can be your own children, your students if you are a teacher, your patients if you are a doctor, your kids if you are a detention counselor. Even simply, your friends and family. Life goes on and on and on. It does before we arrive, continues while we are here, and moves ahead after we are gone. If you improve the life of others – and I KNOW you will, Kara, then that is a great legacy.

Now about your playing basketball. It makes me want to send a warning to all residential homes in the United States, and maybe even all over the world. It would look like this:

BREAKING THE RULES

WARNING TO BASKETBALL TEAMS EVERYWHERE:

KARA WILL BE PLAYING FOR COLUMBIA SCHOOL.

WE SUGGEST YOU AVOID PLAYING THAT TEAM BECAUSE SHE WILL BEAT YOU BAD.
BUT, AFTER HER TEAM WINS, SHE WILL THEN THANK YOU FOR PLAYING BECAUSE SHE HAS GOOD MANNERS.

Kara, you are very special, and I am so happy that things are going so well for you. You deserve everything good that will be coming to you as you go through life. And you make me feel really special in your wanting to write and let me know what is happening. I promise to answer every single letter you write.

Finally, this letter really, really, really needs some animal talk in it. Casanova now walks with his head tilted to one side so he can use his good eye to see what is near him. He does fine and is still the boss of the herd. He sure does look funny, though, with his one eye being a solid pink color. But people are the ones to make statements about others who look funny, pretty or ugly. They are also quick to comment on who is good or bad, based on hardly even knowing them. Other animals (people are animals, you know) seem to be more accepting of each other and of the world around them. Perhaps we can learn some things from them, things that would make our world a better place to live.

Hayua, Kara -- Keep reaching for the stars, and keep writing and telling me about it.

Irv West

�֍

Dear Leonora, (appears on Page 23)

When you came to visit me at detention, I had gone out to buy ice melter. I must have missed you by just a few minutes. They didn't tell me that you had come by at first, finally a staff person mentioned it to me.

I very much want to talk to you...even more, I want to listen to you.

I have often thought about you, Leonora, and wondered how you are doing. If things are good, then I would like to know that; if they are not good then I would like to help make them good. You are special, and deserve the best.

Please get in touch with me.

DO contact me, Leonora. I am very happy that you already tried (the visit), but am saddened that I missed you. Perhaps we can have a pizza together and talk... and talk... and talk.... I would like that.

Irv West

Troubled Youth Can Tame Wild Animals

By Irv West, Detention Counselor, Llama Farmer and COFAMH member

Parallax, February 2006

I work at a detention facility for young people. In fact, I have worked around troubled youth for almost all of my adult life, and I've seen many modalities of treatment come and go—from the now somewhat discredited heavy-handed use of phenothiazines, to various forms of behavioral modification, to electroshock therapy. The current thinking includes psychotropic medications. Children who act out, sometimes in response to some pretty horrific home situations, are labeled ODD and are medicated.

When I hear about success stories that do not involve mood-altering medication or behavioral modification, one that frequently crops up as successful in helping young people involves working with animals. Small animals. Large animals. Pet animals. Farm animals. Even the more mature population in prison rehabilitation programs have demonstrated success with prisoners raising and training animals for adoption.

I have also seen it first-hand in the interaction of many 4-H children with my llamas. Some of the kids have deeply troubled relations with their parents, siblings, schoolmates. But they have no trouble relating to a 400-pound llama . . . or to their 4-H peers.

Looking at programs out west, it is quite common to find young people who have great difficulty with their social skills, shift gears when they are presented with the challenge of taming (giving to and winning trust from) a wild horse. Why? What does a far more powerful 1200-pound horse contribute to a relationship with a stressed young person that we, with all of our intellectual sophistications, cannot provide?

The question has fascinated me for years. It has puzzled me for years. So finally I decided to go to the source — not the animals, but the kids.

At the detention facility where I work, the children have staggered bedtimes and I am often presented with the opportunity to speak with them individually. Without telling the kids what others had responded, I asked eight children (ranging in age from 12 to 16) to shed some light on this "kid-to-horse" interactive phenomenon. Without exception, every child (there was some variation in their choice of language) said, "the animals don't judge us like people do."

Judgment. What a difficult process for any of us to go through, and how painful the process must be for a confused youngster. Judgment is inherently *not* a part of psychotherapeutic relationships, yet I recall when I taught parenting classes, that it *was* an inherent part of most parent-child relations. It played a dominant role in troubled relationships.

Now with my detention kids having isolated for me the "judgment factor" as the successful link in those animal-person relationships, the only thing left for me to do is figure out how to eliminate some of that excess judgment from the parent-child relationship. Perhaps I'll go back to the kids for more advice.

Epilogue

Through all of my years working with troubled youth in this rural area, rarely have I seen a youth admitted to detention who was raised on a farm. Why is this? What might non-farm families take from this rather striking reality that will help their children develop the self-assurance that negates any need to act out, instead building a fulfilling life?

We have an annual county fair that has a heavy agricultural orientation. So I spent the full week there, speaking to farmers and their children. It should be noted that conversations with the kids were in the absence of their parents.

What struck me was the consistency of responses. From adults to children, large 250-head herd dairy farms, to small 30-head herd, they all shared common philosophies.

One boy, no more than 12-years old said, "I like that when I help my dad to plant the hay, then I watch it grow, watch him cut and bale it, then I feed it our cows. It's like a big circle, and I did some of it."

Indeed, this boy might sometimes prefer to not get up an hour earlier before school to help his dad, and spend time after homework mucking out the calf pen. But he is also warmed by knowing that his chores are contributing to the survival of the farm.

What we can learn . . . We can all adapt the lesson by including our children in meaningful family activities. To a smaller extent that same good feeling of responsibility, of contribution, of service is found when, for example, a child is invited to help cook a meal, not just told to clean up after it.

�֎

181

With some exceptions (weather emergencies, for example), farm families eat their meals together. We live in an all-consuming age of electronic communication and with it comes a lack of meaningful dialogue. Facebook is filled with comments like, "I'm awake," "Eating a burger," "Going to sleep." Texting has replaced much of what had been phone conversations or visits. We lose the nuances of face-to-face get-togethers -- the intimacy of being in the presence of the other. Not on the farm. Not while enjoying the harvest of the hard work of parents and children – the bounty on the table.

What we can learn . . . No matter how busy our lives, whether a one- or two-parent household, time must be made for at least occasional meals together. It is a time for casual conversation, but also meaningful conversation.

These are just two examples of how, with all the benefits of modern technology, we need to consciously and deliberately preserve some of the "old" ways. A child needs to have a sense of importance, and parents must work to keep lines of communication open with their children.

Bibliography

APA Working Group, September 10, 2006, "APA Report Sites Critical Gaps in Evidence for Current Treatment of Children's Behavioral and Mental Health Problems," *American Psychological Association.*

Foltz, Robert. Nov 2010, "Medicating Our Youth: Who Determines Rules of Evidence?"

Foltz, Robert, 2010, "Searching for Strengths: Rethinking 'Disorders'." *Reclaiming Children and Youth.*

Horwitz and Wakefield, July 2009, "Should screening for depression among children and adolescents be demedicalized?

Larcada, Liana 2007, "Anti-depressants and Suicidality in Adolescents" *Health Psychology, Pub of Vanderbilt University.*

Olfson, M., Blanco, C., Liu, L., Moreno, C., Laje, G. (2006, June) "National Trends in the Outpatient Treatment of Children and Adolescents with Antipsychotic Drugs" *Arch Gen Psychiatry*

Suggested Reading and Viewing

Reading

Bass, E. and Davis, L., *"The Courage to Heal: A Guide for Women Survivors of Child Sexual Abuse,"* Harper and Row, (1988). A must read book for anyone who has been sexually molested, knows someone who has been, or thinks they do not know anyone who has been (but are almost certainly wrong).

Breggin, P., *"Medication Madness,"* St. Martin's Press, New York (2008). The horrors of over-reliance on psychotropic medications and the marketing mistruths of the pharmaceutical industry. Read his other books as well.

Brooks, Dr. Robert, Read any or all books written by him. Go to his Website and read his published articles and, if at all possible, attend one of his seminars. You will leave inspired, motivated, and the kids you interact with will be the better for it.

Cornell, J. B., *"Sharing Nature with Children,"* Dawn publications, Nevada City, CA (1998). Mind awareness exercises for sharing nature with your children. Geared toward younger children, but teens can easily be the teachers.

De Olivares, J., *"Bring Them Back Alive,"* Taylor Trade Publishing, Lanham, MD (2004). Helping teens get out and stay out of trouble. Down to earth, rational approach by someone who has been on the front lines of the struggle for many years.

Epstein, R., *"The Case Against Adolescence, Rediscovering the Adult in Every Teen,"* Quill Driver Books, Sanger, CA (2007). How we adults contribute to making our teens miserable, and what we should do differently.

Esquith, R., *"Teach Like Your Hair's on Fire,"* Viking Press, New York, NY (2007). Written by a teacher who has demonstrated time and again, that the education process need not fail. He reaches his students employing the same principles I employed to reach my struggling youth – honesty, excitement, the courage to meander off the well-trodden path (that leads nowhere). It's sad that his approach has not become the model for education everywhere. If you enjoy this book, read, *"There are no Shortcuts,"* by the same author.

Faber, A., Melish, E., *"How to Talk So Kids Will Listen & Listen So Kids Will Talk,"* Avon Books, New York NY (1980). It's all about communication between parent and child, and this book is the best guide through that sometimes difficult (especially in the teen years) course.

Kozol, J., *"Death at an Early Age,"* Penguin Books, New York, NY. (1967). Although he writes about his experience as a teacher in the Boston area, all of Kozol's books are an indictment of the education system in every poor neighborhood of this country. Also read *"Amazing Grace,"* *"The Shame of the Nation,"* and his other books. But be prepared to shed tears, and feel rage against the bureaucracy that gives no hope to children who had the misfortune of being born poor.

Mennis, Bernice, "*Breaking Out of Prison*." A guide to self-awareness, consciousness, compassion and freedom – all in the context of the author's experience teaching English in the prison system.

Ryan, William, "*Blaming the Victim,*" Random House, New York, NY (1971). I cherish my copy of this book, which has long been out of print. Nothing I have ever read has given me greater insight into the conspiracy against the poor, through every service delivered to them. Find a copy and read it!

Szasz, T., "*The Medicalization of Everyday Life,*" Syracuse University Press, Syracuse, NY (2007). A series of essays from a psychiatrist considered to be a rebel in his field. The book is written more toward professionals, but stick with it as it tears apart the connection between the medical profession and pharmacological abuse. If you find it fulfilling, then go on to read, "*The Manufacture of Madness,*" by the same author.

Viewing

Freedom Writers DVD. True story that dramatically depicts how one teacher changed the lives of many kids who were beaten down by the educational system.

Precious DVD. There is no better way to experience the struggle of a desperate youth, then through this film. Have a box of tissues nearby, and expect to be deeply moved.

Snow Walker DVD. Here I am exercising writer's privilege. This DVD is not directly relevant to stressed youth, but does speak to how two people, from entirely different walks of life, can come to empathize and respect each other and even learn each other's language. Dramatic, filmed on location in the Alaskan tundra.

Waiting for Superman DVD. I labored over whether to include this film, because I am in conflict about the entire issue of charter schools. This private school approach drains students and funding from the public school system, and exacerbates their struggle to survive. This film shows what can be done -- what has been done -- to provide our youngsters with an education that is both energizing and effective. Most of the principles employed in these charter schools can be duplicated in our public school system, if only they can break away from the chains of inertia, and move toward responsiveness.

Acknowledgements

My own childhood was troubled, with a mother who was in chronic deep depression and a father who was aloof to anything troubling me. "Don't make a federal case," was his most common reaction to my distress. Many of my insights in working with troubled youth, I believe, came from my own upbringing. It was a childhood of constant emotional pain and, until Eleanor and Sam came into it, there was no one there for me. I both closed up and acted out. Had **Eleanor and Sam Seifter** not come into my life, I would have continued to spiral downward. There would have been no youth sharing their lives with me and consequently no book. They were not formally my foster parents, but they did foster me, nurture me, and provide spiritual guidance. They helped me to understand that my life had worth.

Yoshiko Kanzaki was a person with whom I shared a deep love and, in whose arms I was most comforted. I was not worthy of all the beauty, goodness, and grace that she brought into my life. She was taken from this earth far too soon in an automobile accident, and a large part of my soul died with her. She taught me that goodness and caring can conquer evil. I have shared that lesson with many of my youth.

Freida Chapman came later, a very gifted writer and, too, a deeply caring person. Together we raised a son, balancing each other's strengths and weaknesses. I know of no one more giving than she, and my life has been richer for having been shared with her.

Michelle Aleva is a psychologist at a local school and works with many of the kids I have. She responds to them with the same caring that I do, and is permitted into the depths of their souls as I have been. Michelle has often provided me desperately needed support at times of anger and frustration at the system that enslaves our youth.

Sometimes, opening your heart to a struggling youth means more to them than all the therapy and medication you can provide. One person who has opened her farm *and* heart to my kids is **Katrina Capasso** of Dakota Ridge Farms. How many times, I have come there with my detention kids – all dressed in the mandatory detention uniform, and they were immediately put at ease and made to feel welcome. Katrina might have been in the middle of a llama sale, or perhaps a training, but it didn't matter. The impact this had on the kids (for many this caring was a new experience) stayed with them, and we talked about it often. When I run into them on the street, now years later, they still ask about the llamas they met there, and the person who invited them in.

Carol Prevost is the director of a long-term home for detention youth. She had already demonstrated the validity of all that I believe in, all that I have written about here, long before we met. Her caring runs deep and she has been an inspiration to me and to the writing of this book.

This book would not have been written, were it not for the generous offer of editing by **Bernice Mennis**. Bernice is an author in her own right, and her book, *"Breaking Out of Prison: A Guide to Consciousness, Compassion and Freedom,"* explores writing as a path to awareness within the prison system, but also looks at how beliefs, thoughts, concepts, and rules constrict and imprison the spirit.

Another author and supporter is **Paul Pines**. He traveled his own meandering road and came away with insights that are useful in both his personal life and in his therapeutic practice. Paul has "nudged" me toward writing, and has stressed that inherent in these children trusting me rests an obligation to give their voices an audience.

I am grateful to **Chad**, my son, for teaching me how to be a responsive parent, and to his wife, **Christina**, for showing me that there are still people who care on the simplest, yet also deepest levels. She has a genuine purity of purpose. You did well, Chad!

Because I am devoid of computer skills, this manuscript would not have been possible (or at least would have been incredibly frustrating), were it not for **Shannon Rossi** and **Jenny Cooper.** These computer savvy young people were there to make changes, correct my sometimes devastating mistakes and, perhaps most importantly, calm me down and cheer me on. Major kudos also to **Chrissey Dittus** who provided sincere moral support and patience without whose capable skills of making sure everything was where it was supposed to be, this may never have been finished.

The cover art for this book was a collaboration of **Maggie Graf**, a young student artist in the early stages of her career, and **Liz Parsons**, an established artist in Glens Falls, NY. Liz has been immersed in the world of art since she was small. She lived in Portland, Maine for a short period, attending Maine College of Art before returning to New York to continue pursuing her artistic dreams. She can be found on Facebook by searching "Liz Parsons Art."

Finally, and most importantly, I want to thank all of my kids for knowing that I would be there for them, not just while on the clock at a facility but long after. Many of them call me to talk of their fears, their joys and sorrows, their amazing accomplishments in the face of incredible adversity – years after we first met. At the end of each conversation, I am reminded of how privileged I am to have been given this depth of trust, and how hard it was for each of them to bare their soul and expose their vulnerabilities. Their courage is amazing and inspiring. They have been the best teachers.

BOOK ORDER FORM

To order additional copies of this book, fill out this order form (a photocopy of the page is fine) and mail it with a check for $21.95 for each book made out to "Irv West Book" (postage, handling and tax where applicable is included) to:

Breaking the Rules
661 High Street
Athol, NY 12810

To send a copy of the book as a gift, fill out both the information about yourself and the recipient. If you wish, you may include a gift card (or note) to the recipient, and we will be sure to include that with the book. To send multiple gifts, include the additional recipients on a blank piece of paper.

Your Name: _____

Address: _____

_____

Zip: _____

Home Phone: ( ) _____

E-mail: _____

Send a gift copy to:

Name: _____

Address: _____

_____

Zip: _____

Home Phone: ( ) _____

Recipient's E-mail: _____

I have enclosed a check for: $ _____